STORE DESIGN
Experience-Based Retail

Edited by Brendan MacFarlane

images
Publishing

CONTENTS

PREFACE

This is a book about the new developments in using interior design to create experience-based retail stores.

People live in an era where storytelling is becoming essential to product marketing. It seems that this new phenomenon of the experience-based store that can tell a story around the product has become a key issue for innovation in retailing. People all love a good story and want to think what they own or are about to own is also part of a shared experience connecting to other values. Such a store makes us feel like we are entering into another world. These other worlds have become central to experience-based shopping.

It is interesting to think, like many previous innovations, that this new form of shopping also has its historical precedents in the theme mall developments of the 1980s and even earlier in the 19th century. However, the twist here is that what is new is that, in reaction to online shopping, there is this recent emergence of the shopping experience. The shift was first pushed by traders who wanted to go back to providing a real hands-on experience of the product and get to know their customer. Yet, the idea is still connected with online shopping. The idea is that, with an experience store, one can go through the store not buying an actual product but, after leaving, have it later delivered directly to one's home.

The experience-based store is imagined by some retailers as a 'new town square,' which is, in other words, a place where people can meet, talk, exchange, spend time, as well as share information and experiences (Figs. 01–02). Here, one does not merely shop for just one thing but maybe multiple different things that could be found just by association. For example, customers might go look for a new pair of pants and end up having a coffee, reading a book, and seeing a film all in store simply because all these things exist together as a part of the shop experience.

What then one wonders will be the new innovations to the shopping experience? Will the store become a stage for even more elaborate shopping fantasies? Will the impact of drone delivery create new opportunities for innovation in marketing? One can easily imagine sorts of revolutionary ideas will transform not only the way we shop but also the way we make our cities and the ways in which we live.

We have seen with pop-up stores that they have a tremendous impact on how the public does their shopping. However, with the experience store, it is as if we have taken this phenomenon and amplified it. People love to see things that belong to a context. For example, if someone wants to buy a coffee machine, then surely it is more interesting to learn the background of the machine, such as who designed it and how it works. Yet, a story alone is not enough. Why not build a space that supports and enhances this story, such as a coffee bar showing the machine at work? Customers can sit in beautifully designed chairs and feel at home as if they have been invited to a special place where coffee is the centerpiece.

01–02 / 826 Valencia Tenderloin Center,
    by INTERSTICE Architects
03 / The LittleBits Store, by Daily tous les jours

03

These are just a few ways in which a designer could create a space to sell this coffee machine for the client. You have created an experience for the potential customer around the product. The product is no longer just an object on a shelf and has come to life (Fig. 03). You have made a scenario not unlike a piece of theater. All the store elements, from decorations to the employees themselves, guide the customer along to provide a rich experience, capturing their imagination. The customer has the opportunity to see and try the product, discuss it, and spend time enjoying it more deeply. All of these qualities are what a great experience-based store should give. Thus, it is the role of the designer in all of this that they need to create the atmosphere for these experiences to happen.

The designer here actually crafts more of a theatrical space where all the usual interior design issues are bought into focus along with the question of inducing an activity and experience within the area being designed. In this book, we can find some wonderful examples by talented designers from around the world on how spaces are designed with an experience in mind.

This is a wonderful book well worth reading, not just for the excellent case studies provided. The book captures a major shopping trend that is unfolding all over the world, opening up a new era in creativity for all—the designer, the merchandiser, and the public as a whole.

INTRODUCTION

Chapter 1 What is an Experience-Based Retail Store?

The experience-based store is a space where the product is presented through an experience designed for the potential customer inside a dedicated space. The experience of the space is the key to the product, which makes it a more valuable sales tool than actually locating the product in a more direct traditional way. In fact, people often go to an experience-based store to see and experience the brand, join in on the brand experience, and afterwards buy the product online. These are places where one can test the product, try it on, and see it work in various situations. These are places where new experiences and interactive technology come together (Fig. 01).

Chapter 2 Characteristics of Experience-Based Stores

The experience-based store has developed quite recently as a reaction to online shopping, bringing back the social interaction within more traditional stores. The experience space is really a new kind of space and no longer just a store, as it presents everything around the products in highly innovative ways. Therefore, the store is no longer about storing and presenting just the product for direct consumption, but

Take also, for example, the space for Headfoneshop in Toronto, Canada, which is themed around an acoustically anechoic room abstracted out into the shelving and concealed lighting system (Fig. 03). Through the design, we can feel the presence of science and technology merging together to achieve the perfect sound experience. The absolute opportunity to test and relax with the different audio products creates an experiential shopping space. It is interesting to see a number of changes from the traditional store interior. Generally, the space has less stuff as this allows isolation of the products and creates a myth around them.

On the other hand, the space is often filled to give the impression of a wondrous space where treasures can be

instead it focuses on showing by association an atmosphere, accented with its own theme, style, events, and other features.

Some of the differences between experience-based retail spaces and more traditional retail stores can be maybe understood in some of the following ways. Often, the space itself will be the only unique example of the product on hand for the customer to experience since, as mentioned earlier, the product can be purchased online and delivered directly to the customer's home

Spaces are often themed carefully around presenting the attributes of the brand and its history, as if this is something to be shared. People love a story, especially one revolving around the history of a brand or family. For example, wine could be sold through the idea that a great wine is like a great piece of art and presenting the wines in a space akin to an art gallery. One can see this approach with the wine shop AR Vinhos in Portugal, a beautiful white space for the exhibition and appreciation of the products (Fig. 02).

discovered. We see this approach in both 826 Valencia Tenderloin Center, where a children's fantasy world is so wonderfully created (Figs. 04–05), and COR Shop in Brazil, where the products are paints and architectural renderings (Fig. 06). Here, it is all about paring down to some powerful and essential colors and associating them with the walls, floor geometries, and furniture. The brand, by showcasing just some of its products, creates its own space and experience that puts the spectator inside the brand in a personal way.

Counters or cash registers in the experience-based store either have disappeared or have been replaced with something else because these features are mostly no longer needed. Compared with traditional retail stores, the customers can spend their time simply experiencing the products. An

extreme example of this kind of new store can be seen in Life Story, a kind of pop-up store where the product concept lies not in the design but the products' audio and visual elements (Figs. 07–09). In order to experience the products, the experiential space is reduced to bare essential for fullest experience of the product. In Her Majesty's Pleasure, the experience area features a place to sit down and relax that welcomes customers into a personal experience around the product. Yet, it is important to note, again there is an indirect association of relaxation and product.

10 / Race Robotics Lab, by Ministry of Design
11–12 / Kki Sweets and the Little Dröm Store,
　　　 by PRODUCE WORKSHOP PTE LTD

10

Another interesting aspect of experience-based stores can be seen in the emergence of spaces designed for flexibility. In Race Robotics Lab, the space can be changed over time to accommodate different events and uses (Fig. 10). The idea is inherent in the product of robotics; they exist within an evolving industry, and accommodations must be available for future technological advancements. What is so interesting here is the notion that permanence is broken, leaving space to be more dynamic.

Also, we see a change in the way the division between staff and customers is broken down as much as possible. The staff, now transformed into a kind of guide for the customers, will lead customers around and introduce the brand to them. Because of this new relation, there is consequently no need for physical barriers as everyone is inside a shared space. Moreover, we see the emergence of a kind of pathway along which these guided experiences can unfold.

Chapter 3 Design of Experience-Based Retail Stores

For creating experience-based retail spaces, designers should keep in mind the following elements. First of all, one needs to glean information from the function of the products and the history of the brand in order to help conceptualize the space. The space must be conceived as an experience with the products. This will then help guide designers in handling different visualization issues in choosing color and materials, thus setting the tone for how the space should be experienced.

Generally speaking, one can see that the goal of an experience-based store is to first introduce the experience. The products are often put into a position of being discovered. The idea is to make a kind of ritual around the product through connections and storytelling. Having done this, the essential experience of the product should be establish and only then is the topic of purchasing presented. This sequence, on the other hand, could easily be inverted so that the spectator is taken back through a journey of discovery.

The interior design is fundamental to this experience and therefore choice of materials, furniture selection, lighting design, color, and details are so essential. The story of what the designer is narrating is then so important in all of these previous choices. For example, we can see quite clearly the story conveyed in the project Kki Sweets and the Little Dröm Store (Figs. 11–12). The all the design choices connect back to the product. The white wooden walls give us a feeling of something light, delicate, and handmade which is related to the products sold in the shop. The choice of a simple gray floor works to reinforce the above mood. Moreover, it is also shiny and clean, much like what is being sold. Lighting is indirect so one sees the pieces on sale more easily, reinforcing this sense of being at home. Proportions are generous here and not crowded like in a traditional store. The shelves look like they could belong in someone's living room. Lastly, the details are simple like what is sold, minimal and not fussy. If designers are in touch with these elements of storytelling in their design, then they will create a store providing a rather magical experience for customers.

CASE STUDIES

ChicBus Alipay Flagship Store

Location / Hangzhou, China
Area / 1722 square feet (160 square meters)
Completion / 2017
Design / LYCS Architecture
Photography / Elton, Hu Xianjuan

Aiming at building a closer relationship between technology and life, the store is a collection of technology products. The design team explored the spatial design strategy of laying tension on visitors' experience within the store. By revealing the contrast of fantastic futuristic spaces and traditional human feelings, designers portray the collision of the future and tradition to create a retail store.

By connecting the real and virtual world, the store reveals its space by oblique dividing the site. The cutting line, also acting as the principal axis, divides the space into two different sides, and maximizing the effect of this collision between the virtual and the real. In addition, the cutting line guides customers into the space by its oriented features. With the invisible partition, which extends from floor to ceiling, the two sides offer totally different experiences of illusion and reality. The clearly divided sides are designed for different kinds of products, one side displaying the new, and trendy technology products while the other side displaying more traditional fashion-related products. Though the bright 'virtual space' is clearly distinguished from the dark 'real space,' the integrality has been kept by the integration of the flowing lines.

In the high-tech zone composed of light-colored matrix, the showcase and the transparent glazed surface reveals a sense of future. The extensive dark plywood-clad zone for traditional products, together with its brass features, contributes to a real space for raw industrial materials. The lighting is organized in terms of different atmospheres. The lighting system for the 'virtual space' is placed in line with the cross lines of the matrix, intensifying the matrix, thus creating a bright 'virtual space.' In addition, by using the metallic drop lights and lighting embedded in the dark plywood cabinets, the 'real space' brings visitors a traditional homely experience.

01 / Virtual space

① Virtual space
② Physical space

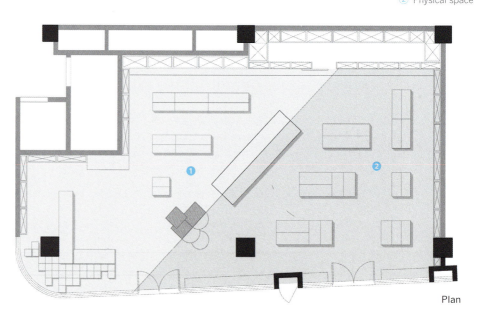

Plan

02 / Virtual and physical space
03 / Dividing line
04–05 / Details of products in virtual space

Race Robotics Lab

Location / Singapore
Area / 2616 square feet (243 square meters)
Completion / 2017
Design / Ministry of Design
Photography / CI&A Photography—Edward
Hendricks Owner

The client commissioned a design company to design the branding and spatial experience. The interior space is designed for a new robotic facility aimed at educating and introducing robots into automating existing manufacturing industries. The client intended to also feature a series of interchangeable modular robots as a key unique proposition. Inspired by the concept of modularity as well as influenced by aesthetics of precision and dynamism, the logotype is an expression of a complete form comprised of individual standalone parts.

The brief for the laboratory space required flexibility to showcase a changing series of modular robots as well as be used for training and lectures. The laboratory needed to be a continuous open space, yet conducive for small clusters for hands-on training. Underpinning this brief, designers also sought to create an engaging and future-forward spatial experience that denotes the idea of industrial automation and precision.

Upon arrival at the lift lobby, a vivid prelude to the laboratory space greets the viewer. A web of soaring white lines cut through the black space to create an anamorphic experience to disorient the floor from the ceiling. From the black envelope of the lift lobby, an oversized door pivots open to reveal a dramatic metallic faceted space, creating a contrast that is at once striking yet complementary. For maximum flexibility to the space, designers developed to seamlessly create a dynamic space by deconstructing the ceiling and wall planes into an array of dazzling facets. Each facet comprises stacked layers of hollow hand-cut aluminum tubing; rotating the direction of the tubes with every facet to create a bold multi-directional effect. The aluminum screen cladding also serves to cloak the necessary but unsightly mechanical and electrical services while allowing ease of access for operation. This skin was shaped in plan with enclaves for small group work clusters accompanied by separate access hatches to the services behind. The random sprinkle of custom LED strips serves to highlight the multi-directional panels with a cutting-edge aesthetic. Overall, the space provides a suitable future-forward backdrop to usher in an age of automation and robotics.

01 / Exterior space
02 / Stacked layers of hand-cut aluminum tubing

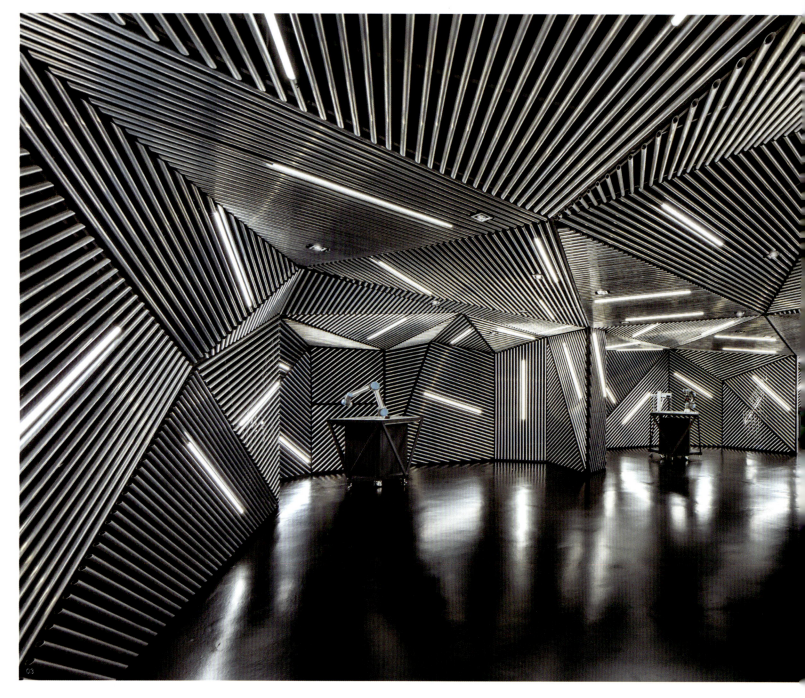

03 / Interior space
04 / Service hatch

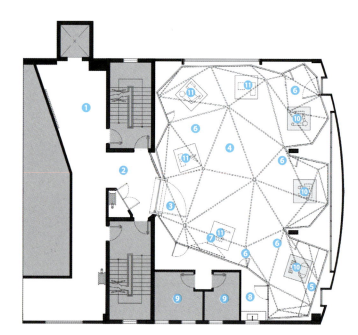

Plan

1. Lift lobby
2. Entrance vestibule
3. Entrance
4. Teaching/lecture area
5. Display counter
6. Service hatch
7. Projector screen
8. Storage room
9. Restroom
10. Robot station
11. Extra robot station

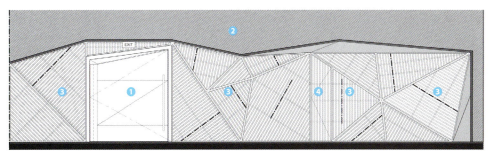

Elevation

① Entrance
② Ceiling space
③ Aluminum screen panel with LED strip
④ Service hatch

04

Chic Bus Stop

Location / Hangzhou, China
Area / 388 square feet (36 square meters)
Completion / 2017
Design / PUMP DESIGN Ltd.
Photography / Zhou Kai

Clothing and jewelry stores geared for women are a common sight, whereas women-focused tech stores not so much. The designers aimed at designing a tech store that would appeal to women of all ages, especially for young women. The theme of the design used was 'Flying Saucer in Tiffany Blue.'

When customers walk in the store, the designers wanted to take them into a blue sea. The store is a lovely blue flying saucer irregularly shaped with an arc. The main entrance side is with radian angle. A bus over the logo seems to welcome customers to this beautiful new world. The main operator's desk is on top of a large circular LED lamp, and the lights around it extend eight circular mirrors with their own apertures to meet the needs of different customers. The saucer has no walls, and all sides are lined with Tiffany blue panels in a neat and vertical arrangement. The spaces between the boards allow light to penetrate and create a relaxing atmosphere while ensuring visibility. There is an access on the opposite side; the plate is seamless horizontal connection, with the logo embedded in the plate, strengthening the brand concept. The vertical panels, like flying saucers, are not closed, and the horizontal ones look like closed doors, as if the saucer is waiting to take off.

The hull of the flying saucer is made of transparent glass as a partition from the outside world so that the inner and outer parts form a synergy. There is no such thing as a ceiling. There are eight fine steel frames, which converge into a center, surrounded by two circles of steel frames, much like the roof of a castle in a fairy tale.

01 / Central display table and hanging mirrors

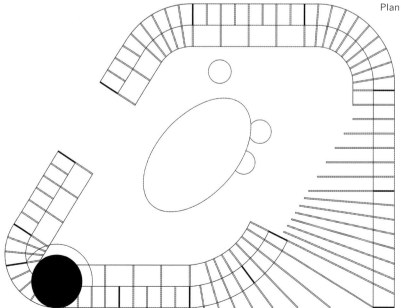

Plan

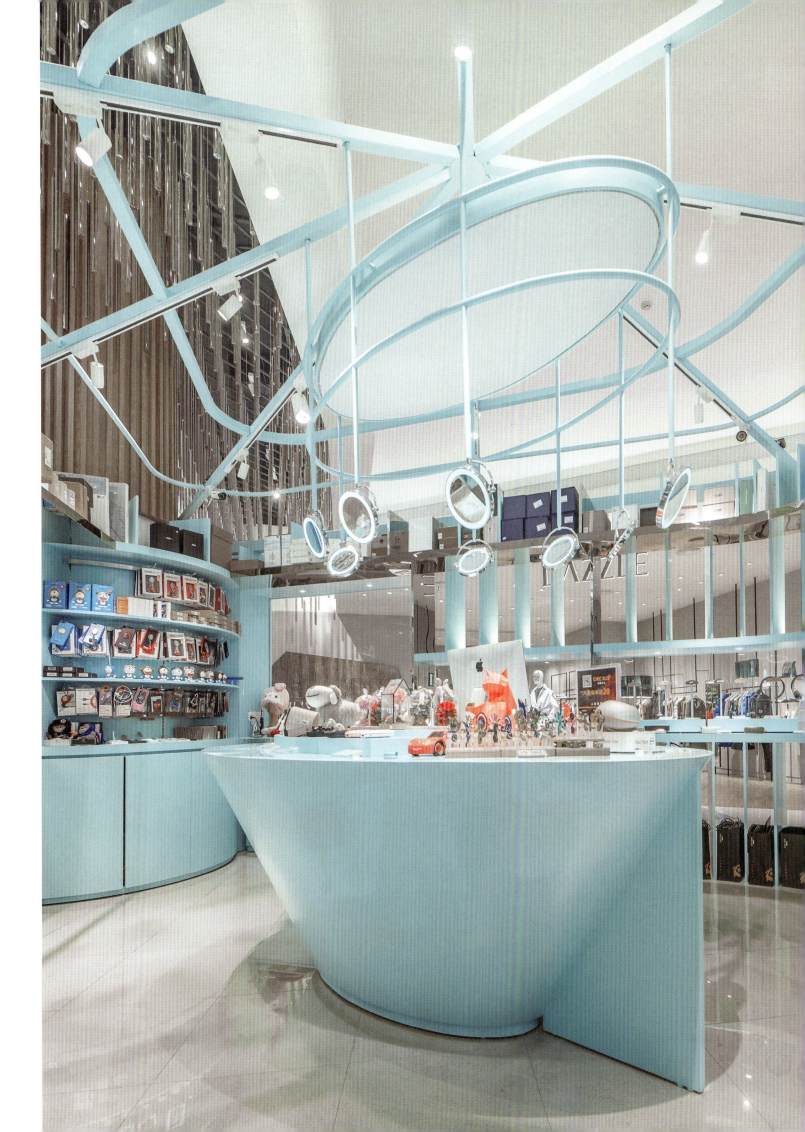

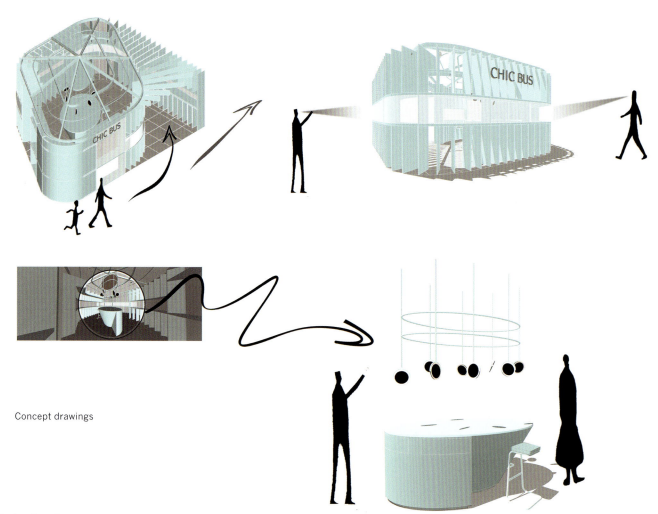

Concept drawings

02 / Exterior view of store
03 / Main entrance
04 / Structure that looks like a blue cake

Headfoneshop

Location / Toronto, Canada
Area / 300 square feet (28 square meters)
Completion / 2017
Design / Batay-Csorba Architects
Photography / Doublespace Photography

The store is designed for sales of high-end headphones, earphones, amps, and audio accessories, located on the main floor of a 42-story mixed-use tower with direct subway connecting to Toronto's Yonge and Sheppard station. The owner of the store is a passionate audio expert who challenges the typical retail store experience of focusing solely on the product and efficiency of the transaction for maximizing turnover. Instead, the design objective was to celebrate the ritual of listening to music and the process of testing audio equipment.

The intimate, dark, and tactile atmosphere gives customers a quiet lounge-like atmosphere to relax while listening to music. It is not uncommon for customers to spend several hours pairing systems and listening to music. Dark smoked oak millwork and herringbone flooring, sensuous velvet upholstery, soft amber lighting, and patented brass fittings create a dark and subdued palette that curate a subtle, moody ambience. In contrast, powder-coated folded metal panels, secured with brass screws to wrap the ceiling and walls, producing a spatially dynamic and immersive space that mimics the intense and enveloping audio experience. The metal wrapper in one sense is aggressive but the scale and repetition produce a subtle movement and flow. The juxtaposition between strength and softness creates a composition of emotional tones felt on the body.

While the design strives to affect how a customer feels, it also rethinks how the environment can optimize the product. Instead of the product display system being a separate element with the architecture, it dissolves the boundary between object and architecture. The headphone stands were designed as a wall display that extended over the customers and down the opposite wall, enveloping them in the display itself. The bent metal plate allows for display of headphones in multiple configurations, while hiding unsightly wires.

01 / Display wall

Axonometric drawing

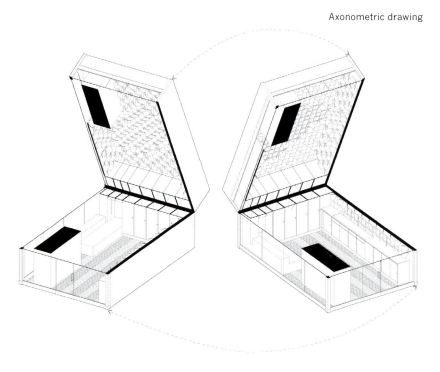

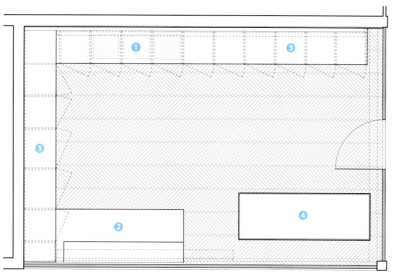

Plan

1. Display case
2. Lounge seating
3. Storage cabinet
4. Building structure

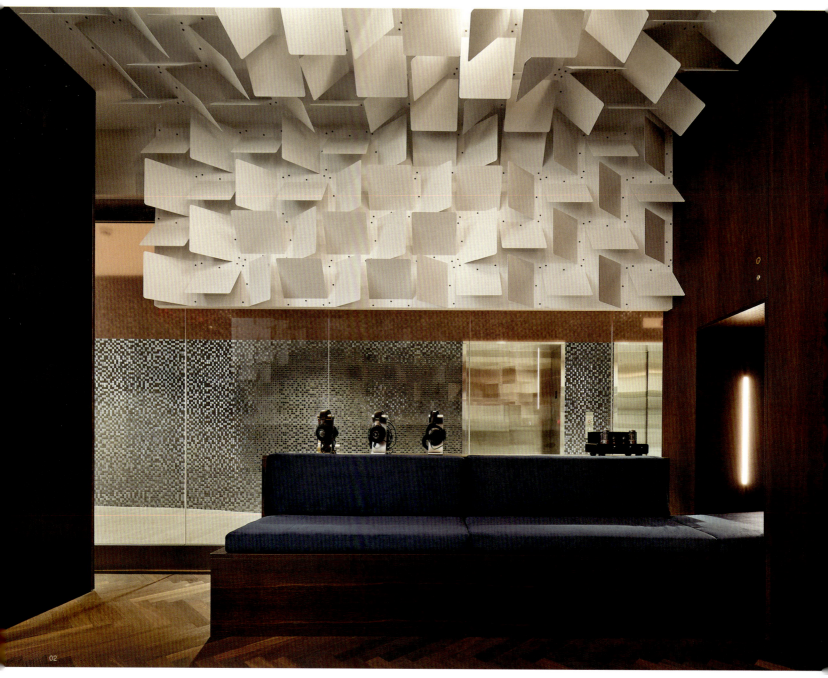

03 / View from entrance
04 / Signage
05 / Display case

The LittleBits Store

Location / New York, USA
Area / 2500 square feet (232 square meters)
Completion / 2015
Design / Daily tous les jours
Photography / Raymond Adams

The store creates a customized retail experience driven by imagination, innovation and play, translating the intimate experience of creating and learning into a large-scale collective experience. It is a pioneer of technology retail stores. Customers can make projects on site and leave their inventions in the store for others to remix or buy. The products in the store are the inspiring electronics products, which are changing the way people live.

01 / Display of key products
02 / Musical twister

The store includes an area with interactive installations for people to get inspired by existing inventions, a workshop to create inventions, and a place to share them with the world. In the front of store, interactive displays showcase ready-made contraptions with step-by-step instructions, allowing customers to assemble their own version in the store or at home. Visitors are invited to grab an instruction card and make their way to a workshop table where they can create, play, and remix.

The store served as a lab for consumers and as a classroom, allowing them to further reinvent themselves, the retail experience, and the world around them. For the interior design of the store, designers conceived everything in the shop as modular, giving the store team the flexibility to constantly reinvent their retail experience by curating workshop sessions, talks, play days, or any other special events to animate and transform the space for a few hours at a time. The store becomes not only a platform for people to discover the product but also for the store team to further understand their own product and how it creates meaningful interactions with the world.

Plan

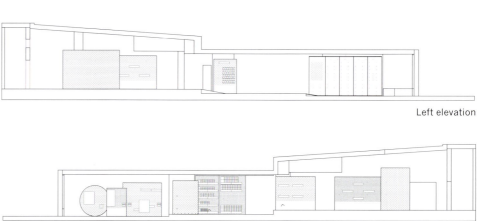

Left elevation

Right elevation

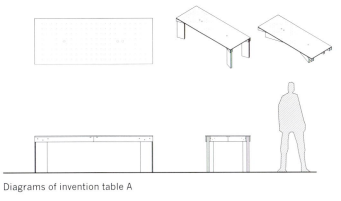

Diagrams of invention table A

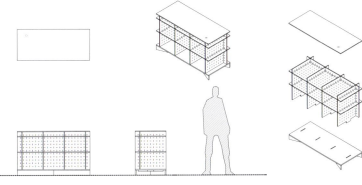

Diagrams of checkout counter

03 / Entrance and musical twister
04 / Workshop for creation and learning
05 / Wall of accessories
06 / Photo booth for inventions

Disha Electrical and Lighting Store

Location / Chandigarh, India
Area / 1892 square feet (176 square meters)
Completion / 2015
Design / Studio Ardete Pvt Ltd.
Photography / Purnesh Dev Nikhanj

The store is located in the heart of the electronics and electrical market in the city of Chandigarh. The design brief was not only to reinterpret the store as an up-scale electrical showroom, but also to expand it to encompass decorative and outdoor lighting fixtures. In essence, the challenge was to rebuild the whole space with additions without changing the context.

As a solution the space is divided into two zones. The front zone deals with electrical equipment and the rear zone is designed as a space to display decorative and outdoor lighting fixtures. These two zones are connected via a passage that acts as a buffer, separating and yet binding the two zones together. Both of these spaces are conceived as independent and individual entities with a common underlying design sensibility. The first zone is a study in contrasts with its grey background tone superimposed by fluid white forms that begin at the ceiling but drop down to become a part of the walls—movement caught and frozen in space. In addition, green elements are used in juxtaposition with wooden paneled display units for electrical equipment to enliven the interiors. The passage connecting the two zones uses mirrors to pique the curiosity of the visitor. The somber, dark theme of the passage contrasts perfectly with the highlighted interiors of the front zone. Housing unique light fixtures, the rear zone is carpeted, from floor to ceiling, in black. An irregular, zigzag volume designed to display fixtures, sits in the center of the space. Fiber optic cables with dynamic lighting are hung from the entire ceiling thus exuding sophistication.

The ceiling consists of wooden panels arranged in random and geometrical patterns with a single light fixture being the main element. The furniture is kept in dark tones to match the flooring of the display center. A meeting room is also included in the showroom, featuring fabric panels with backlit crystal lighting. A white section of the false ceiling flows down and transforms into a conference table in an offbeat design solution.

01 / Glimpses of interior to draw in customers
02 / Unconventional furniture and displays enhancing space

03 / Central passage leading to mirror
04 / Semi-covered discussion area
05 / Green storage areas

05

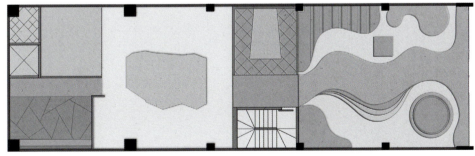

False ceiling plan

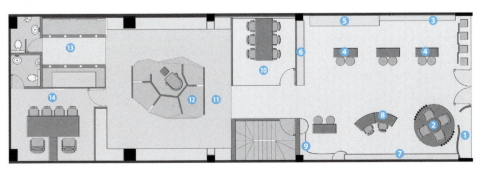

Layout plan

1. Show window
2. Discussion area
3. Wall lights display
4. Display counter
5. Switches display
6. Fan display
7. Decorative lights
8. Billing counter
9. Downlighter display
10. Meeting room
11. Lighting experience center
12. Chandelier display
13. Outdoor lighting display
14. MD cabin

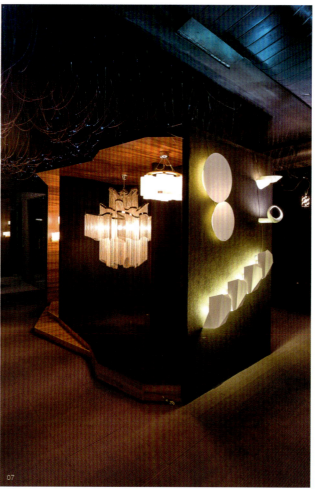

06 / Display lighting with darker tones
07 / Zig-zag designs unifying space
08 / Each fixture with own display treatment
09 / Cabin with beige tones and dark furniture

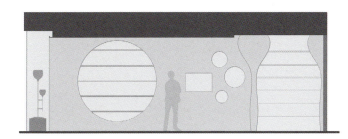

Elevations

Flos Scandinavia Showroom

Location / Copenhagen, Denmark
Area / 5382 square feet (500 square meters)
Completion / 2017
Design / OEO Studio
Photography / Michael Anastassiades, Piero Lissoni,
Jasper Morrison, Achille Castiglioni, Pier Giacomo

Located in an old tractor repair workshop amongst spacious former warehouses of one of Copenhagen's old industrial docks, the showroom has been entirely transformed to create a bold new spatial experience with an international feel that allows the products to take central stage. The design company worked with spatial elements that draw on the structure of the building itself, which is monolithic, and contrasting elements that inspire curiosity, bringing the products to life and creating a dynamic interplay between architecture and home lighting.

A playful sculptural staircase works as a dramatic display element and as a zone divider within the open space. With its bold appearance, the staircase triggers curiosity and works as a perfect backdrop for the products. Another important design element is the Cover House, a separate home lighting display area within the showroom, clad with brick from Danish brickwork manufacturer, Petersen Tegl. The masonry was carefully selected by the design company to create a perfect contrast and to give emphasis to the lighting products. The showroom features many unique architectural details, including bespoke shelving units and an innovative display system that offers a new approach to display lighting. The display system has been designed so that it can be configured in multiple ways, offering a perfect system to showcase lighting solutions and to create a subtle and inspiring spatial backdrop.

The main inspiration of the design was the structure and history of the old building, the contrast of materials, and the interplay of natural and artificial light. Designers have worked with spatial elements that draw on the body of this wonderful old industrial building. Monolithic and contrasting structures have been deployed to create a play of light and shadow, an ambiance bringing iconic products to the center stage.

01 / View from exterior
02 / Showroom arrangement with symmetry

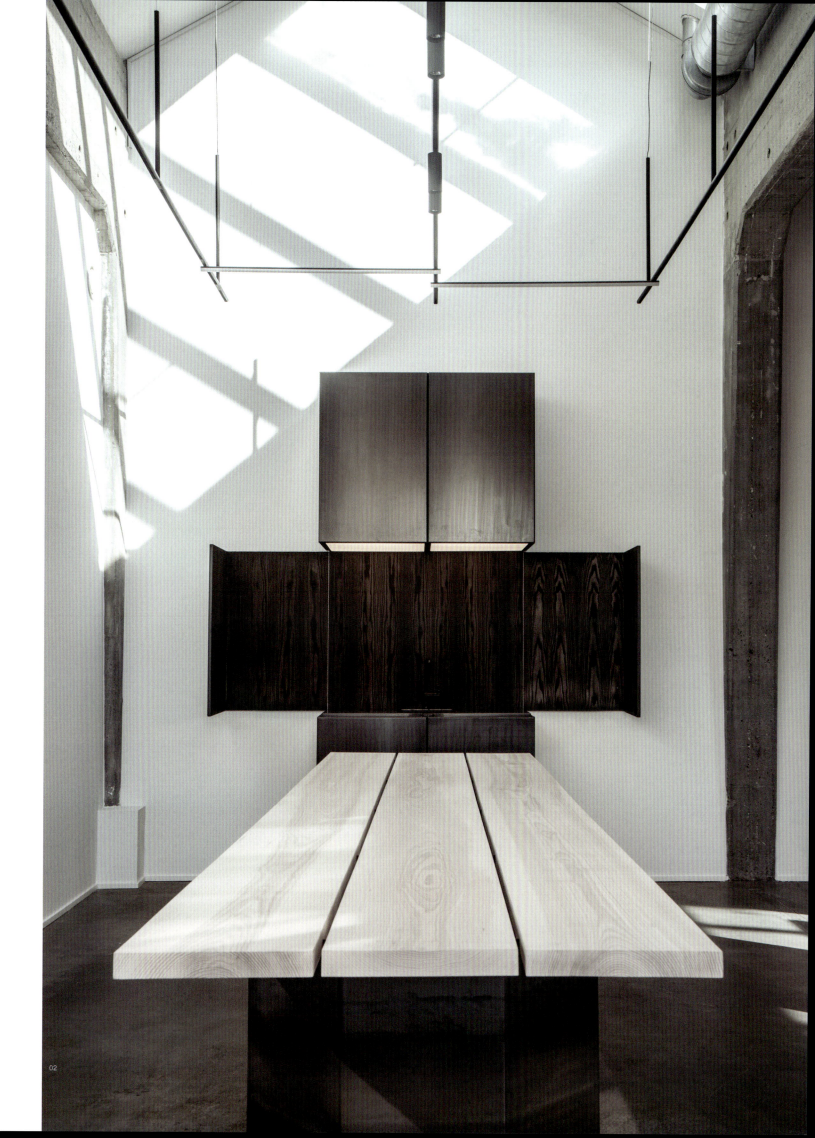

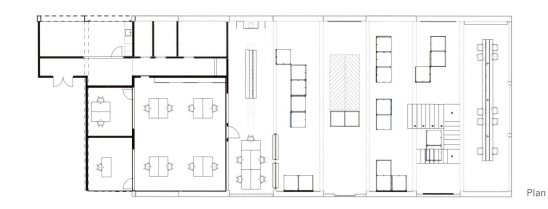

Plan

03 / Lighting arrangement
04 / Interior of store
05 / Floor lamp
06 / Staircase in showroom

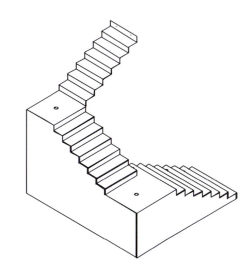

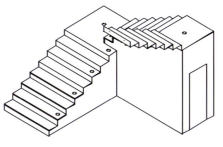

Details of staircase

UNILUX

Location / Beirut, Lebanon
Area / 861 square feet (80 square meters)
Completion / 2015
Design / SOMA
Photography / SOMA

The existing space provided a unique opportunity for a commercial street front fit for a lighting showroom. The client, the largest supplier of high-end light fixtures in Lebanon, requested a unique space in which to exhibit the products sold by the company. Due to the shallow depth of the existing main space, a conscious decision was made to envision the space as larger than the confines of its walls in order to visually appear larger as well as draw pedestrians into the store.

What started as a simple two-dimensional system evolved into a sophisticated matrix that guided the design process throughout the space? By envisioning the space as a solid mass, designers were able to carefully craft the negative usable space with incredible flexibility. This mass was thought of as larger than the confines of the walls, only to be sliced by a new glass storefront, effectively engaging the 'fourth wall' of the sidewalk. By utilizing a parametric script, this mass manifests itself as a series of uniform white cubes that envelope and unify the space. The result is a matrix of geometric elements carved and crafted to create a dynamic and inhabitable space in which users can interact not only with the light fixtures themselves, but immerse themselves in the interaction of the light along the complex surfaces.

The basement provides a more intimate setting in which products are displayed. Inspired by this cellar appearance, the various light fixtures are displayed in a series of niches along the narrow basement corridors. While the walls and floor are rendered in a highly reflective black, the niches are rendered white so the individual characteristics of each light fixture are displayed. The result is a mosaic of different colors and shades of light expressed in their individual niches, reflected in the floor and ceiling. Advanced parametric tools were used in the showroom in order to array 1000 white glass-reinforced plastic cubes, creating one continuous surface within the space. This innovative main room was also designed to be used in tandem for events and features a separate bar area that fits seamlessly into the room's design.

01 / Lighting showroom hall

① Existing building
② Showroom
③ Display room
④ Electrical room

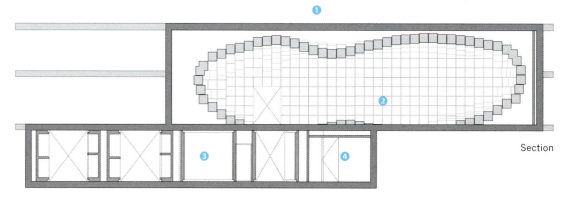

Section

02

03

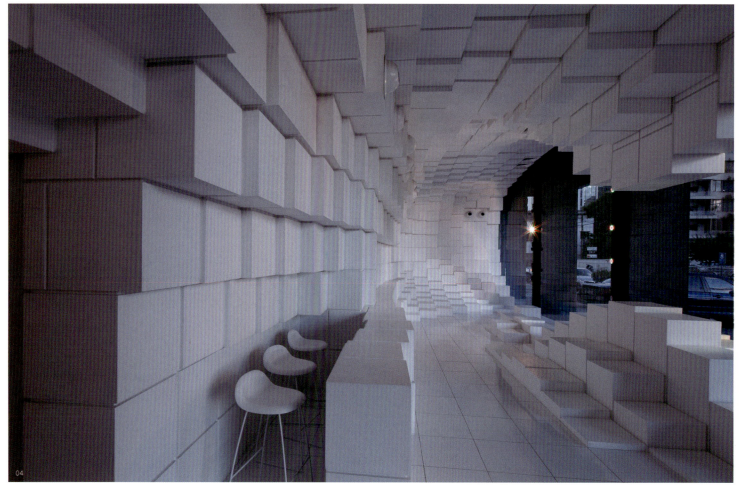

04

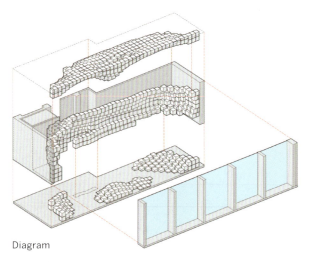

Diagram

1		BRW(1)
2		BRW(2)
3		TRW
4		TRB
5		TRF
6		C5
7		C1
8		BW1
9		MW1
10		TW1
11		C6
12		C2
13		BW2
14		MW2
15		TW2
16		C7
17		C3
18		C8(1)
19		C8(2)
20		W3
21		DOOR
22		C4
23		W4
24		BLB
25		BLF
26		BAR
27		BRB
28		BRF
29		BML
30		BMR
25		TLF

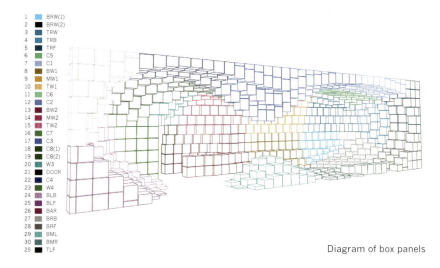

Diagram of box panels

① Showroom
② Bar
③ Corridor
④ Reception
⑤ Catalogue
⑥ Kitchen
⑦ Restroom
⑧ Partner's office
⑨ Manager's office
⑩ Meeting room
⑪ Entrance to basement

First-floor plan

Basement plan

① Display room   ⑤ Storage
② Elevator room   ⑥ Electrical room
③ Material room   ⑦ Entrance to first floor
④ Vestibule

02 / Storefront
03 / Space sculpted by light
04 / Reception area
05 / Lighting showroom

05

Portugal SERIP Lighting Exhibition Hall

Location / Beijing, China
Area / 4628 square feet (430 square meters)
Completion / 2017
Design / CUN Design
Photography / Wang Ting, Wang Jin

The designers got rid of traditional rules and integrated diverse styles, such as minimalism and modernism, into the interior design. The design inspiration stems from the lamps of the brand, which have round, spiral, and irregular shapes. Good design had to be customized rather than applied uniformly, since each space has its own characteristics.

The building itself, with its colored steel tile structure, integrates with surrounding buildings. The original site lacked conditions of being an independent brand store. Lamps bring distinctively different display effects in the daytime and at night. Thus designers used beams of light to cut the area into black and white spaces. In the black and white area, the designers respectively created some artificial light with the products. In the black area, a number of crystal lamps were displayed to show off each lamp's lighting abilities; while in the white area, lamps with artistic shapes were displayed, such as unique hand-blown glass lamps. As for the façade, the designers used the slices in the façade to hide the whole building, instead of strengthening the building itself. The white slices formed the main view of the hall. Under sunlight, the shadows from the slices change over time.

Moreover, since no entrance was designed, the whole exhibition hall has a sort of independence. The designers have added some gray walls in the space, which helps to form separate independent areas between the black and white spaces.

01 / Entrance
02 / Light box

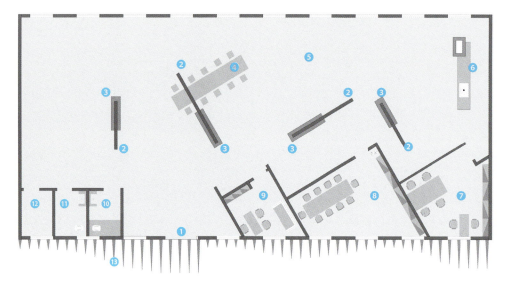

Plan

1 Hall entrance
2 Lamp display wall
3 Light box for display
4 Counter
5 Exhibition hall
6 Service desk
7 Design department
8 Meeting room
9 Office
10 Women's restroom
11 Men's restroom
12 Switching room
13 Architectural
appearance

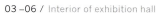

03 –06 / Interior of exhibition hall

Her Majesty's Pleasure

Location / Toronto, Canada
Area / 2799 square feet (260 square meters)
Completion / 2014
Design / +tongtong
Photography / Lisa Petrole

The store is a place designed to bring customers an experience combining beauty salon, café, retail boutique, and bar. Architecturally, the space seamlessly reflects this multi-purpose program, blurring the lines between each zone. By reiterating materials, patterns and concepts across each area, the store is cohesive and connected throughout the space. Overall, the design firm kept the palette light and fresh, selecting white, light grey, charcoal, and varying shades of blue for the main color scheme. Hits of copper, bright yellow, Douglas fir plywood, and slate added warmth and highlighted the palette. A bold custom-design graphic floor pattern of blues and grey tile energize the entry of café and bar.

The one side of the room consists of a seemingly ornate, yet stripped down, whitewashed bar topped with white marble. A line of geometrically folded copper stools reflect the coved lights under the bar. The designers accentuated the towering ceilings by installing industrial, multi-pane glass and steel window frames behind the bar, a treatment that plays with the space's proportions and also allows patrons to view into the salon area from the bar. The bar and the salon are mirror images of the other, with identical white enameled steel pendant lights hanging in parallel.

Entering the store, the eye is drawn to the architectural structure at the back of the space. Serving double duty as a pop-up retail boutique and reception to the salon, the monolith is a product display system grown out of the architectural construction. Traveling past the wooden pop-up, customers arrive in the beauty salon. The marble bar from the entry wraps around, extending the experience into the salon and setting the stage for manicures. Patrons sit at the marble bar as they get their hair done, with bartenders serving on the other side. Located across the aisle, the makeup lounge, which can be used to collect oneself after a treatment or booked for private functions, is articulated from the rest of the space as a wood cabin. At the center of the lounge, geometric copper stools surround a custom-designed table, which is topped with copper and white diamond-shaped tiles.

01 / Exterior of store
02 / Bar

01

Plan

1 Entry
2 Juice bar
3 Color bar
4 Color selection wall
5 Pop-up store
6 Lounge area
7 Pedi-patio
8 Make-up lounge
9 Blow-dry bar
10 Preparation area
11 Retreat room
12 Office
13 Hair wash area
14 Washroom
15 Staff lounge
16 Storage room

04–05 / White counter and ceiling lamp

06 / Racks for display
07 / Wood cabin
08 / Wide window providing light
09 / Area for sitting

Le Manoir in Montreal

Location / Montreal, Canada
Area / 1330 square feet (124 square meters)
Completion / 2016
Design / TUX
Photography / Maxime Brouillet

The store is an avant-garde boutique offering beauty services and fashionable clothing. In an effort to maintain a youthful brand image and expand the retail aspect of the business, the client mandated the design company to create a new store layout and update the interior design. The designers wanted to tell an inspirational, hopeful and influential brand story to customers, which is just what the brand pursues.

The main challenge of this project was to create an environment that would be flexible in functionality, yet allow for versatility and customization in terms of aesthetics. With a holistic approach, designers proposed a multi-scale solution through work that incorporates everything from a considered new layout and spatial organization to a refined design, using millwork with sophisticated finishes. With a holistic approach, designers proposed a multi-scale solution through work that incorporates everything from a well-planned layout and spatial organization to a refined design, using millwork with sophisticated finishes. In order to display the brand's multipurpose products, the concept behind the floor plan was an open-space layout with the welcome desk being in the center of the space. This elegant, multifunctional core piece serves as a service area, a waiting area, and a retail space combined. The use of natural stone as a key texture elevates the brand image and establishes a sense of professionalism through a luxurious and polished feel. Ultimately, the material palette and the construction details generate an overall look that is classically timeless, yet feels unique in its richness.

Since its official reopening at the end of 2016, the store has seen great success and its photogenic environment has become a natural backdrop for social media users. The designers and clients hope this fresh and modern retail space continues to become part of the street's natural backdrop and commercial scene.

01 / White cabinet, table, and chairs

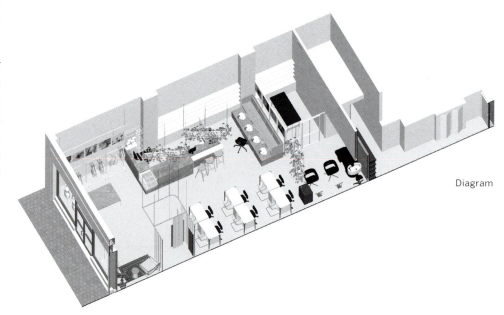

Diagram

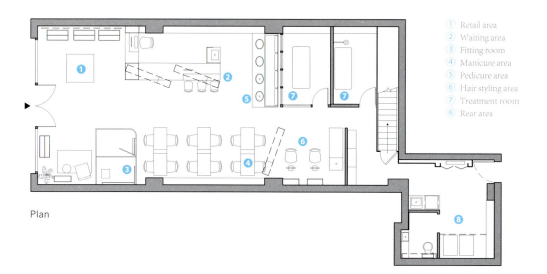

Plan

1. Retail area
2. Waiting area
3. Fitting room
4. Manicure area
5. Pedicure area
6. Hair styling area
7. Treatment room
8. Rear area

02 / Interior of store
03 / Reception area
04 / Pedicure area

03

04

Boutique Zazz

Location / Quebec, Canada
Completion / 2016
Design / Hatem+D
Photography / Maxyme Gagné

The store is located in Quebec. Involved in the strategic positioning of this new banner, the design team created a new concept, and fully designed the branding and the web content in a complete and all-inclusive design for the boutique. The store was a project in which designers could dare to have fun, both in the concept and its substance. The interior design showed an inspiring and feminine environment as well as an euphoric, girly and sparkling atmosphere.

The store wanted to create a customer experience in which paths lead them through stations displaying different product arrays. The general concept is built around the linearity of hair, which is reinforced by custom-made chain curtains that divide different sections for products, thereby creating a distinctive feature. Those curtains are also used on the mezzanine to give privacy in an area reserved for hair and wig stylists. Every element is custom-built, from furniture to lighting and other unique signage for the boutique. Every detail is analyzed: the white, the iridescence, the transparency, the linearity. Shapes, colors and textures are used to put emphasis on products and focal design points like the front desk and the stairwell. The ceiling height is used to purify the space.

Because of ingenious lighting, an impression of effervescence can be felt throughout the store. From the outside, the shinning and glamorous design of the mirror arch and the full-height window boutique invites the customer in. With its creative and sparkling features, the boutique distinguishes itself and synergies with every aspect of itself. The boutique embodies the concept of architectural branding: a unique and recognizable space where the coherence of architectural aspects crystallizes the value of the brand.

01 / Exterior of store
02 / Interior of store

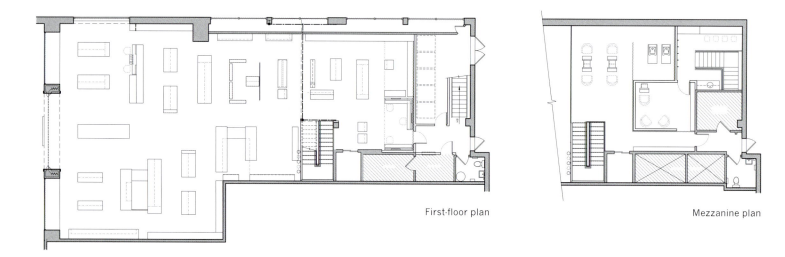

First-floor plan

Mezzanine plan

03 / Racks from ground towards ceiling

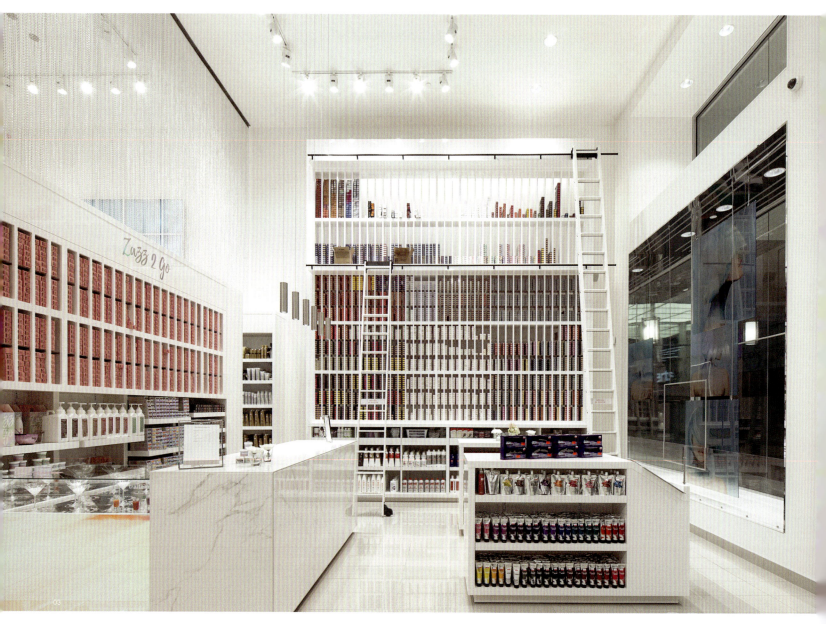

04 / Staircase
05 / Product display

Zanadu Traveling Experience Space

Location / Shanghai, China
Area / 6458 square feet (600 square meters)
Completion / 2016
Design / Shishang Architecture
Photography / Sui Sicong

Zanadu is an online travel agency in China. It established this space for an offline experience so that customers can personally experience their traveling products.

The store embodies the brand and has much functionality. Popular destinations and traveling products are displayed with VR technology. Considering that users need to wear VR glasses, private areas were designed so that customers can experience the travel products without being bothered. This design concept is the travel agency of the future. Currently, tourists in China book online. However, this travel experience store can provide customers with an offline experience to entice customers into purchasing particular products.

The design is filled with technical elements. The interior space looks like a pixel landscape. A digital cloud is suspended from the ceiling, and digitized cubes scatter the entire space. The pixel elements represent the online attributes of the brand and are perfectly integrated into the offline environment. Five huge digitally stylized hot air-balloons are placed in the center of space, inviting visitors to sit in them and begin a virtual journey. The 20 cubes with touch screens around the space represent 20 destinations, each showing different journeys that the customer can book. Projection screens and surround system provide the customers with audiovisual effects as if they are in a theater. Everything in the store is linked to the customer management system via QR code. Each visitor can experience VR or access a specified product by scanning a QR code.

01 / Interior of store

Plan

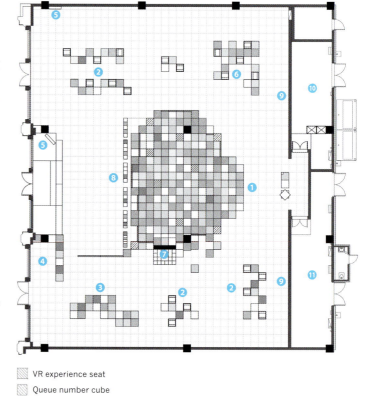

① VR experience entrance
② Product display area
③ VR glass experience area
④ Checkout counter in gift shop
⑤ Poster display board
⑥ Luxury product display area
⑦ Control area
⑧ Zanadu logo
⑨ Projection screen
⑩ Storage room
⑪ Employee lounge

▨ VR experience seat
▨ Queue number cube

02–03 / VR experience area

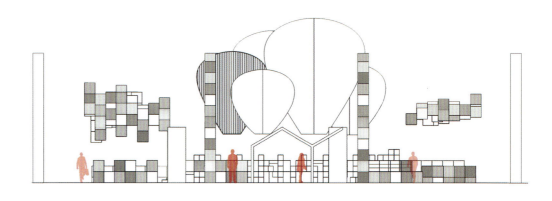

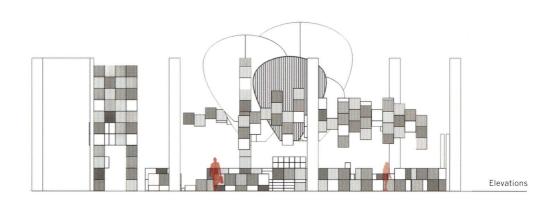

Elevations

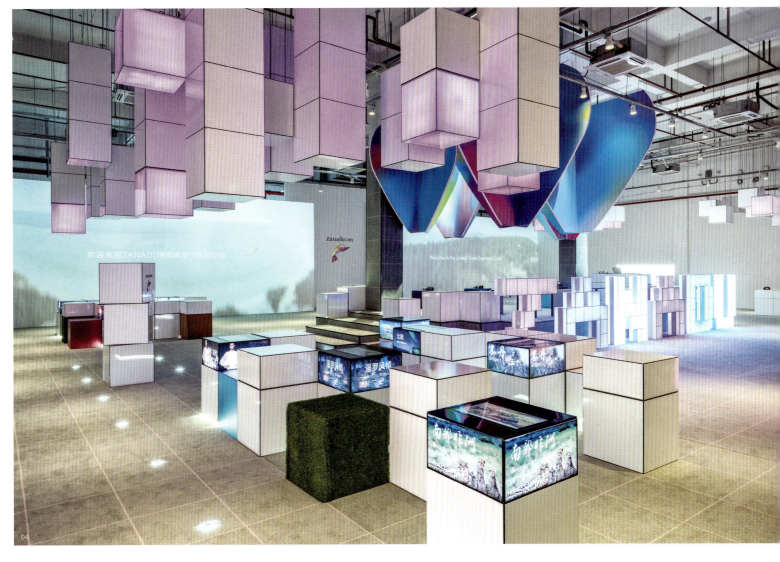

04 / Product display area
05 / Entrance
06 / Luxury product display area and projection screen

826 Valencia Tenderloin Center

Location / San Francisco, USA
Area / 5200 square feet (483 square meters)
Completion / 2016
Design / INTERSTICE Architects
Photography / Matthew Millman

The center recently opened its doors in the heart of San Francisco. The client worked with a design company to expand a non-profit project. The center was awarded the Special Commendation Award for Social Responsibility from the AIA San Francisco's 2017 Design Awards Program.

The store with its unique retail experience is dedicated to supporting young students in developing their creative and expository writing skills as well as helping teachers inspire their creativity through writing. The new location establishes an extraordinary and transformative place welcoming to children. The interactive structure in the interior space was created to provide the children an experience space for self-expression through creative writing. It is a magical store where children pass through the door in the store and enter into a fantastic space decorated as tree house. Secret ramps and passages are arranged in the tree house. The store is divided into many functional areas, such as offices, workshops, conference rooms, and the tree house itself for resting.

Large windows are installed in the façade of the store so that interior space is full of light. The reception area is at the entrance and many lockers have numbers. Goods are hung on the opposite wall of the reception desk. The store has realized a truly transformative project in a community where it was so desperately needed. The community came together to invest in design for social impact. The project not only reinvigorated and strengthened a dilapidated building, but its true influence can be felt on the streets and in the homes of the surrounding community, just starting to realize the project's creative power.

01 / Storefront
02 / Reading nook with access to treehouse balcony

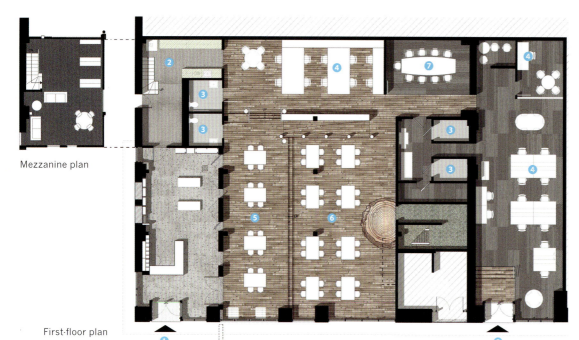

Mezzanine plan

First-floor plan

03 / Storefront glazing acting as display languages for cultures
04 / Interior retail environment for curiosity
05 / Wall of doors connecting entrance with studios

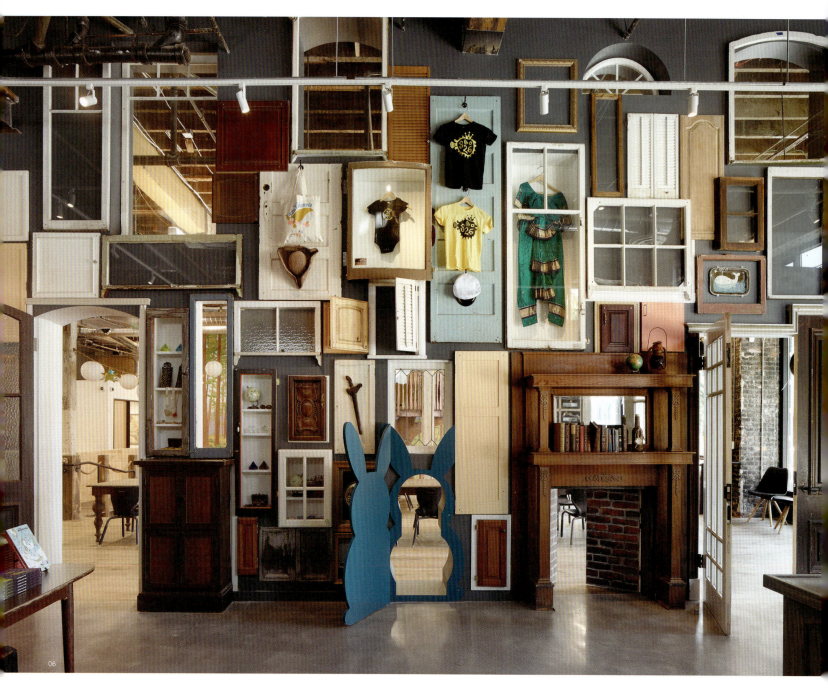

06 / Wall of doors stimulating children's creativity
07 / Overall view of writing workshop space
08 / Private niches where children can work
09 / Interior reading nook with rope ladder to treehouse

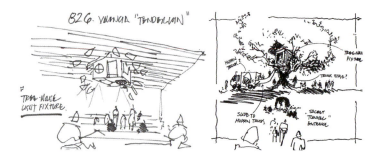
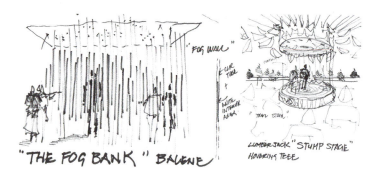

Sketches

Martian Embassy

Location / Sydney, Australia
Area / 1615 square feet (150 square meters)
Completion / 2012
Design / LAVA (Laboratory for Visionary Architecture)
Photography / Brett Boardman, Peter Murphy

The store was designed as an immersive space of oscillating plywood ribs brought to life by red light and sound projections. This interior design is for The Sydney Story Factory, a non-profit creative writing center for young people in Sydney.

The design is a fusion of a whale, a rocket, and a time tunnel, inspired by the stuff great stories are made of. The concept is to awaken creativity in kids, so the design acts as a trigger, firing up the engines of imagination. It is an intergalactic journey, from the embassy, at the street entrance, to the shop full of red planet traveler essentials, to the classroom. By the time kids reach the writing classes, they have forgotten they are in school. Designers used a fluid geometry to merge the three program components, which are embassy, school, and shop, and a computer model was sliced and nested into buildable components. 1068 pieces of CNC-cut plywood were put together like a giant puzzle. Using technologies from the yacht and space industry, the timber ribs create shelves, seats, benches, storage, counters, and displays and continue as strips on the floor.

Edged with Martian green, the curvy plywood flows seamlessly so that walls, ceiling, and floor become one element. A mix of Martian essential oils inspires young imaginations, whilst the sounds and lights of the red planet animate the space. Martian passports, alien money, cans of gravity, abduction kits, and SPF 5000 sunscreen are just some of the 'Made on Mars' gift products sold in the store.

01 / Interior of store

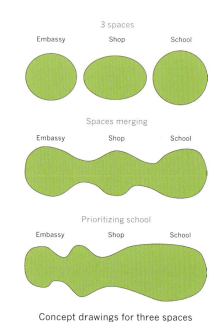

Concept drawings for three spaces

Longitudinal section

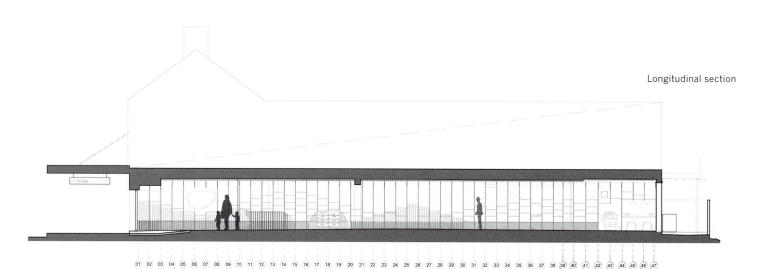

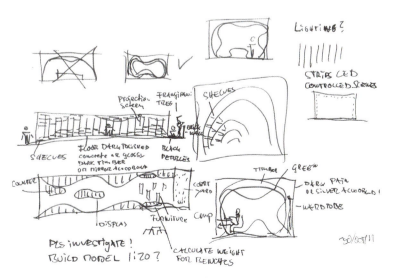

Sketch 1

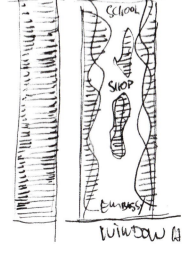

Sketch 2

02 / Unconventional classrooms
03 / Interior of classroom
04 / Panorama of store

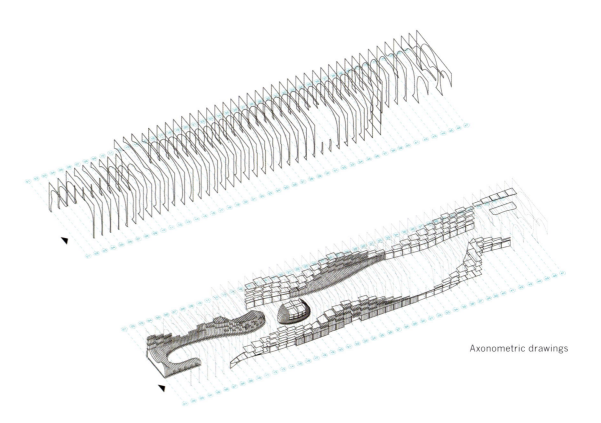

Axonometric drawings

Alcomag

Location / Kiev, Ukraine
Area / 2207 square feet (205 square meters)
Completion / 2017
Design / Azovskiy + Pahomova
Photography / Andrey Avdeenko

Alcomag is a new commercial network of alcoholic beverages in Ukraine. A great opening of the whole network started in Dnepr, one of the biggest cities of Ukraine. The client wanted the design company to create a concept of the shop, then find a location and adapt the existing design.

All the preparatory work for creating the interior design went very quickly and, after a few weeks, the designers started implementing of the project. After a successful implementation of the project, the design company received an offer to create another project for Alcomag, but this time in Kiev, the capital of Ukraine.

The designers Oleg Azovskiy and Anna Pahomova created a comfortable shopping environment that makes the customers willing to return again and again. Racks have been arranged in the interior space for maximum convenience and space efficiency. For optimal display of goods, all the products have been placed orderly on the racks for the buyers. Besides the high shelves, low shelves are also arranged in the store. Designers allocated a place for a tasting room, which is located near the panoramic windows. The customers can sit, drink, and experience the products in the area before purchase.

01 / Wine room
02 / Tasting area

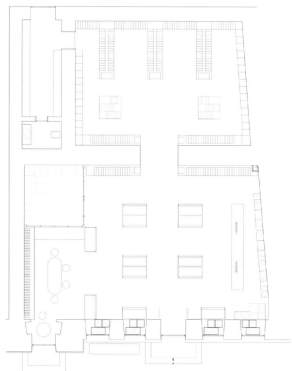

Plan of Alcomag Dnepr

03 / Racks with beverages
04 / View from tasting area
05 / Checkout area

06 / Tables in tasting area
07 / Checkout counter
08 / Wine racks and stands

Plan of Alcomag Kiev

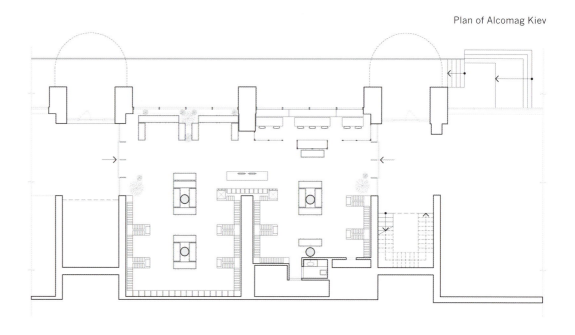

AR Vinhos

Location / Aveiro, Portugal
Area / 753 square feet (70 square meters)
Completion / 2014
Design / Paulo Martins Arq&Design
Photography / Ana Tavares

Located in a high-standing residential block, this wine shop intends to be a cutting-edge outlet that treats wine in an exclusive manner, concerned with the way that it is displayed, offering a unique experience to its customers.

Green decoration at the entrance of the space is an allusion to the vineyards. The focal point becomes a flowing plane, which guides the eye through the space, passing by the exhibited wine bottles and ending at the main counter. The wine house is divided in two floors: the top floor with a more private space, where wine tasting and workshops can be conducted, and the first floor dedicated to the commercial activity of the shop. As the shop covers two floors, it was critical to create an intense spatial and conceptual continuity, which could contribute to a strong and unified image of the intervention. On the lower floor, the designers placed the customer attendance counter and storage areas of the shop, while the upper floor was dedicated to premium attendance, where older wines and spirits cohabit with a table for tasting events or simply personalized tasting sessions.

Based on minimalistic and pure lines, this wine house project is characterized by a plane that is at the center of the design, which flows around the entire space. The plane knit these two complementing spaces together, which unfolds and adapts to the space, like a scarf blowing in the wind, a simple symbolism of freedom and nature. The effect is further reinforced by a green horizontal plane. This plane not only brings the spaces together, but, at the same time, is both the service counter on the ground floor and a display case on the upper floor.

01 / Front view
02 / Counter

03

03 / Wine cabinet on second floor
04 / Tasting area
05 / Premium wine showcase

First-floor plan

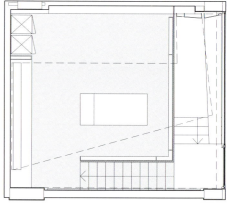

Second-floor plan

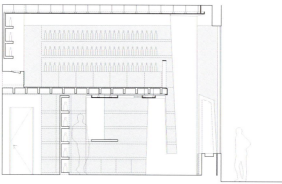

Section 1

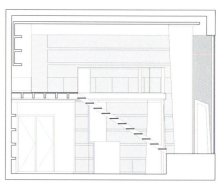

Section 2

04

05

Mistral

Location / São Paulo, Brazil
Area / 1367 square feet (127 square meters)
Completion / 2012
Design / Studio Arthur Casas
Photography / Fernando Guerra

The wine retailer Mistral presented the design company with the challenge of creating a store that would innovate the way their clients approached the wine world. Most of their sales are done through the internet, thus the task was to conceive a space that would showcase the wine in a recreational way, justifying the physical presence of the store and by attracting both new customers and connoisseurs.

The store is relatively small for the extensive program: sales space, cellar, storage, interactive gallery, reading room, and wine tasting. Adopting a curve seemed to be the natural solution in order to integrate this multiplicity by evoking the sensorial perceptions of the wine. Designers aimed to invite customers to discover the unique content of each bottle. The curve creates a path where the spaces are gradually revealed. Seemingly floating bottles follow the organic shape, formed by a backlight topped by a wooden lath, giving the store an elegant and discrete atmosphere. A dark stripe conceals several screens that are lit through the touch of white bottles placed within each section, revealing general information. All the technical equipment was hidden within the walls. Separated from the main corridor by an automatic glass door, a double-height cellar has its own air conditioning system to store rare wines. An interactive table was designed to showcase a monthly selection of wines, with sensors underneath each bottle allowing the related content to be projected on the table screen. The bottle becomes a cursor, when twisted, information, such as location, interviews with producers, and notation, appears.

In the rear of the store, a reading space was created with books in between the wooden laths that extend to the floor. At every space, the bottles are presented in surprising ways. Even though omnipresent, the object is never monotonous, as it becomes a texture that follows the context of each ambiance. Wine holds sensations and stories that are extremely diverse; suggesting this multiplicity of possibilities in discovering the content of a wine bottle was the starting point of the architectural project. The innovation of this project consists on trying to bring together architecture, product, information, and interaction into one single entity.

01 / Exterior of store
02 / Curve creating a path where spaces are gradually revealed

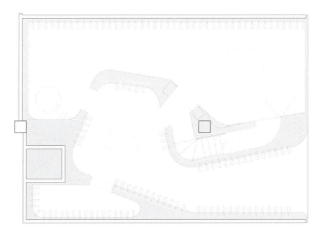

First-floor plan

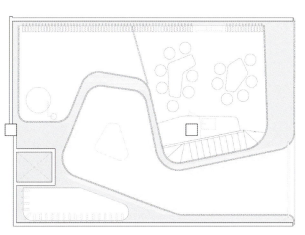

Mezzanine plan

Rocky Pond Winery Tasting Room

Location / Washington, USA
Area / 2000 square feet (186 square meters)
Completion / 2016
Design / SkB Architects
Photography / Benjamin Benschneider

The winery is designed to bring a heightened sense of awareness to the winery's story and their wines. The tasting room serves as a sophisticated venue in which to relax and celebrate the experience of wine, while staying true to the humble, agricultural surroundings of the area.

01 / Entrance and outdoor seating area
02 / Bar with pewter countertop

Reworking a speculative retail space, the existing façade was transformed via a new, fully open storefront system, merging a small, semi-enclosed exterior patio with the inside. The owners' interest in focusing on the experience of wine finds its expression in the casual seating arrangements and the subtle, natural materials and hues used to build out the space. The space is a custom-fabricated, pewter-topped tasting room, which is set atop a whitewashed pine base. Opposite the tasting room, an art piece designed by the architects merges cartographic imagery of Burgundy with photographic imagery of vineyards. The piece serves as homage to the owners' wine tasting bike trip through France that served as the inspiration for the winery.

Neutral tones take precedence, with whitewashed pine used for wall surfaces, whitewashed oak for flooring, and natural fir for ceiling surfaces. Bar cabinetry is a mix of white oak and dark paint. A small, private tasting and dining area can be created through the use of a set of folding walls, which can isolate a portion of the space. Lighting and C-channel ceiling divisions are blackened to provide a visual contrast to the natural tones that otherwise dominate. A small catering kitchen, restroom, and basement storage area are round out the back-of-house areas. A set of vitrines inset into the wall next to the private tasting area showcase a cross-section of earth and vines taken from selected vineyards. Each vitrine highlights the varying grape vines and soil compositions found in the winery's vineyards. The exhibit serves as a reminder of the natural processes needed to transform grapes into wine as well as a way to educate guests about the soils and climate that make the wines so special.

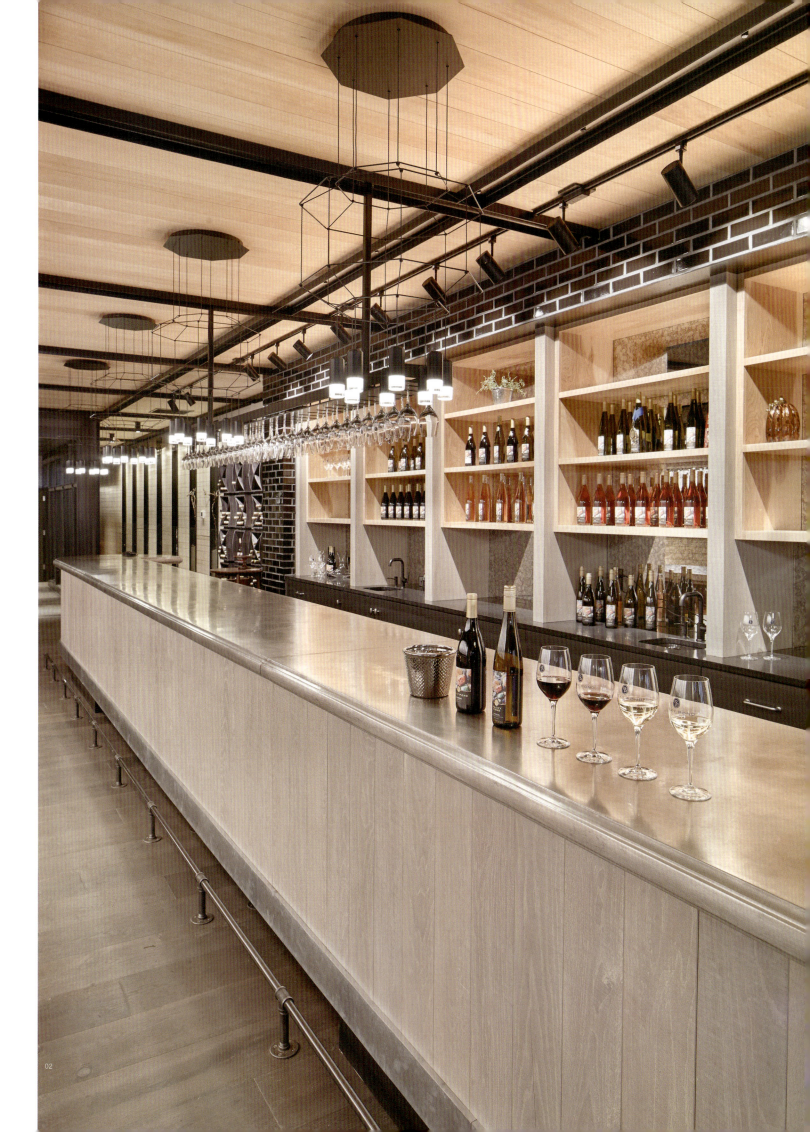

03 / View towards tasting room
04 / Seating arrangement throughout space
05 / View towards restrooms and rear of store
06 / Glass vitrines containing grape vines and soil
     for brand storytelling

Plan

① Entry
② Tasting bar
③ Private tasting room
④ Gallery
⑤ Storage room
⑥ Restroom

Showroom Albert Reichmuth

Location / Zurich, Switzerland
Area / 1399 square feet (130 square meters)
Completion / 2010
Design / OOS
Photography / Christine Müller

The store, designed for sales, wine tasting, and seminars, is aimed at appealing to regular customers and passers-by alike. The intent of the interior design was to present an image of wine cases. Some wine cases even cover the entire room up to the ceiling, creating a cave-like environment.

The wooden cases are simultaneously an architectural element and a part of the furniture. Arranged in a grid pattern, they serve as a platform for wines, books, seating areas, and illuminated table display cabinets. The mostly French wines are spatially divided into various geographical regions and groupings, which conceal specific histories, cultures, and landscapes. The reception counter is located in the middle of the room and is equipped for wine consultation. The counter's violet and ruby colors provide quite a contrast to the wood of the wine cases. The lights on the ceiling formally illuminate the wine bottles and integrate themselves into the presentation of the bottles.

Across from the sales venue's showroom is a sitting room with a small kitchen. This section is used as the wine store's reception room for tasting and seminars for up to 15 people. The spatial layout continues here and allows the cave-like wine-case landscape to slowly taper off. The wine collection depot in the inner courtyard has also received a facelift. With a light-colored façade and new lettering on the walls, the building blends into the inner courtyard and incorporates the existing design elements of the wine store's corporate design.

01 / Exterior view
02 / Showroom integrating with urban neighborhood

Plan

03 / Counter for both reception and wine consulting desk
04 / Colors of reception counter contrasting with wood of wine cases
05 / Seminar room

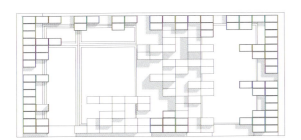

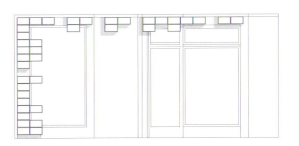

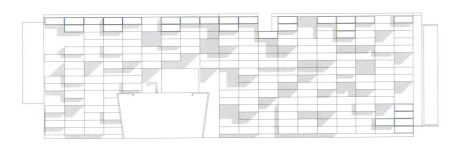

Sectional view of wooden boxes

Vinos & Viandas

Location / Valladolid, Spain
Area / 377 square feet (35 square meters)
Completion / 2017
Design / Zooco Estudio
Photography / Imagen Subliminal

The design of the wine cellar is characterized by a series of wooden arches, which evoke ancient underground cellars. The designers employed the arches to serve as a central motif, alluding to wooden barrels of wine cellars, bottles of wine, and antique vaulted cellars. The juxtaposed arches spatially define the venue both vertically and horizontally, forming a dynamic store for exhibiting, tasting, and browsing a refined collection of wine.

The designers carefully chose materials that would magnify the experiential qualities of their store. Wood is used for the ribs system, implying the wooden barrels of wine vaults. Stone is used for the flooring, alluding to antique cellars and mirrors are used to generate amplitude and an atmospheric world of reflections. The concept of this space comes from exploring the familiar world of wine. In our imaginations, there are a lot of these references. Thus, the designers attempted to abstract these images in a manner fitting the site's circular shape. The circular shape is noticeable in many ways, such as in wooden wine barrels, in wine bottles, and in antique wine cellars. Therefore, the circle introduces people into this world as the leitmotif of the project. The juxtaposition of several circles in the transversal and longitudinal direction of the local creates a space where the required situations appear, such as the counter, tasting table, and exhibition space. This chain of curves originates a series of arches of the space that linearly will be seen as vaults, a constructive system that evokes the ancient underground cellars.

To complete the space, it is necessary to mention the different materials. There are three materials in this project: wood is used for the rib system, stone for the floor, and a reflective material that a world of reflections where those circles seem to contain some kind of liquid.

01 / Interior of store

1. Entrance
2. Folding table
3. Counter
4. Cellar
5. Kitchen
6. Restroom

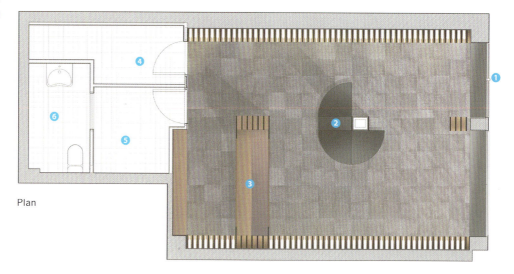

Plan

01

02 / Entrance
03 / Wooden arches
04 / Folding table

05 / Custom-designed display area

Section

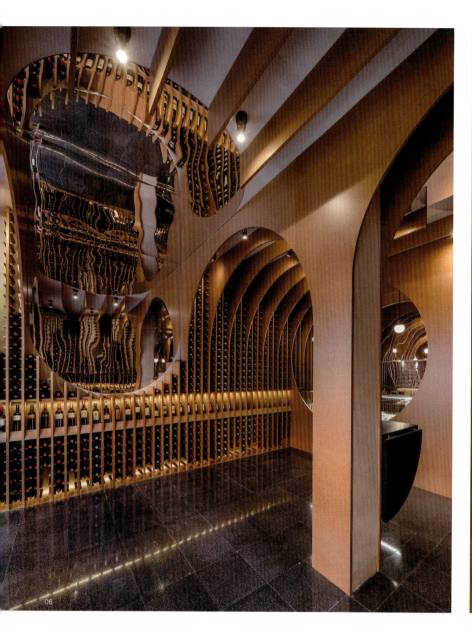

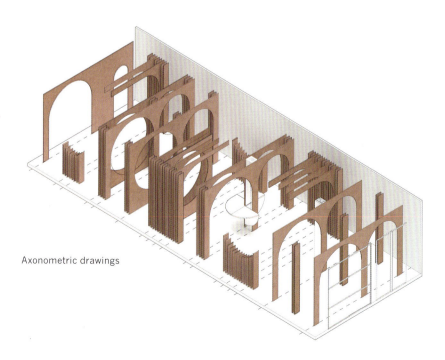

Axonometric drawings

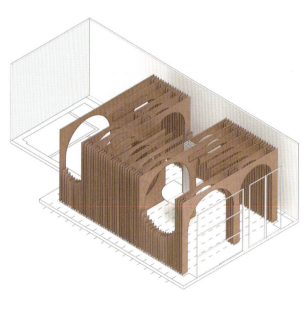

06 / Mirrors or display shelves reflecting products
07 / Details of shelves
08 / Counter in store

Oak Panels Wine Shop

Location / Rotterdam, Netherlands
Area / 2153 square feet (200 square meters)
Completion / 2016
Design / AAAN
Photography / Sebastian van Damme, Adriaan van der Ploeg

This new wine shop is located in the center of Rotterdam. The four-story shop has been transformed into a modern and warmly finished space clad with laser-engraved oak panels.

01 / Storefront
02 / Detail of engraved panels

The continuous space is flanked by two cabinet walls with niches, cupboards, and amenities. Wine boxes are stored inside the cabinets, and large cutouts function as displays for over 300 different bottles of wine. Service areas, like storage, toilets, and an office, are concealed behind the wall. The result is a clear and spacious shop with a strong focus on the wines. The cabinets are clad with oak panels, which are engraved with labels of famous and desirable wine houses. The rear walls of the wine display cutouts show the original brickwork originating from the foundation of a 17th century VOC shipyard (Dutch East India Company). The shop consists of four levels: a basement, first floor, mezzanine and second floor. In addition to the main retail space, the shop features a small bar, a kitchen, a tasting area, and a cellar. The low-lit wine cellar has an intriguing atmosphere, while the other floors are bright and generous. Careful integration of daylight from above balances the perception of the entrance and the mezzanine in the back.

All furniture is custom-designed. In the cellar, two long black cabinets filled with fine gravel contain luxurious wines. A large cabinet with integrated cash register is placed on the ground floor. A small bar is placed on the mezzanine to accommodate small tastings. The first floor is used as the main tasting area for larger groups and contains educative tables with maps of wine regions engraved in the tabletops.

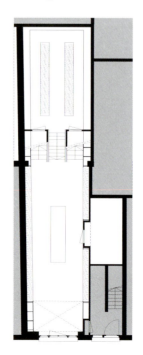
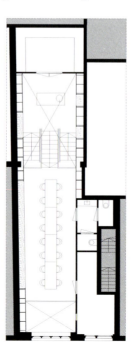

Plans

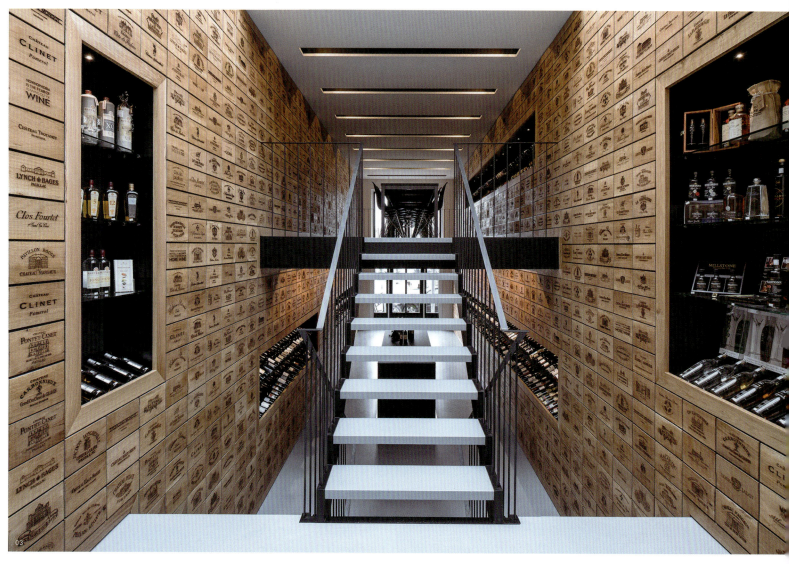

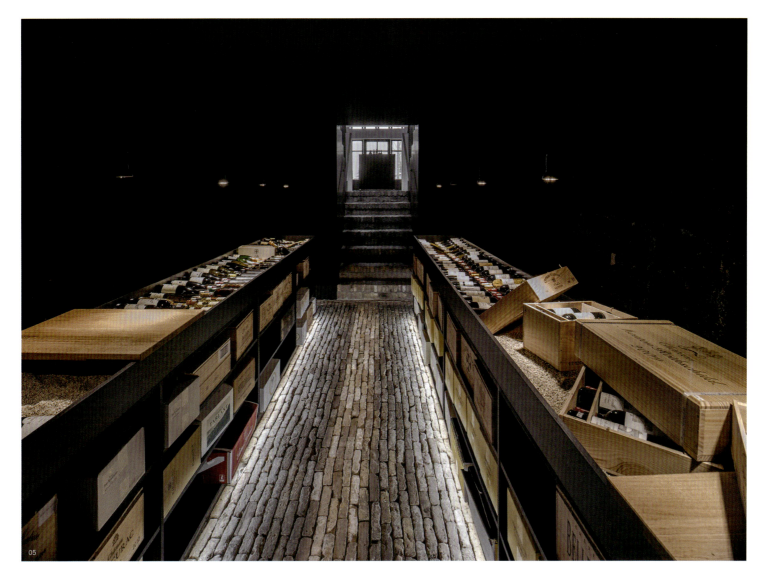

03 / Interior of store
04 / Tasting area on second floor
05 / Cellar

Sections

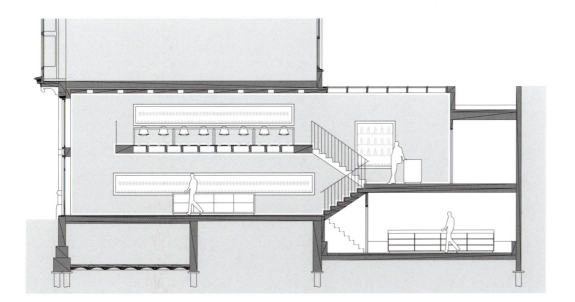

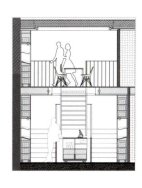

Artopex Store

Location / Montreal, Canada
Area / 12,000 square feet (1115 square meters)
Completion / 2015
Design / Lemay
Photography / Claude-Simon Langlois

Artopex, one of Quebec's largest manufacturers of office furniture, commissioned Lemay to design its new space in Montreal. The project is located in the prestigious former headquarters of the Royal Bank of Canada. After sitting vacant for more than 25 years, the emblematic building has been completely revitalized and rethought in order to give this brand a space that reflects its image and values.

The project aimed at more than displaying products and the goal was to communicate the manufacturer's history and identity with a graphic and spatial narrative thread, with the ultimate objective of preserving memories and emphasizing the quality of its products. The idea of territory emerged as the central theme for the entire interior design concept. Starting at the entrance, an uninterrupted ribbon of images of Quebec landscapes guides visitors through the different zones of the space, spread across two basement levels. Quebec's urban, industrial, and natural landscapes translate the brand's commitment towards the community and the environment into two values at the core of the company's culture. The pixelated treatment of the background images creates a defocused effect that directs the eye toward the product, making an original contribution to its display.

From the outset, the designers faced two major challenges: the front door is dwarfed by imposing neoclassical columns, and the showroom's basement location suffers from a shortage of natural light. In response to the first, an enormous LED-animated marquee draws the gaze and energizes the entrance with a variety of lighting effects. To address the second, a large opening in the floor leads to oversized wooden stairs serving as a meeting place as well as a display space, while flooding the lower levels with natural light. The arrangement of the different zones, linked by lighting effects, creates several contrasting ambiances that enhance the visitors' experience. The new space becomes a tool for creative product display. Normally seen at the individual scale, furniture is experienced in relation with the environment.

01 / Entrance
02 / Showroom with wooden stairs

01

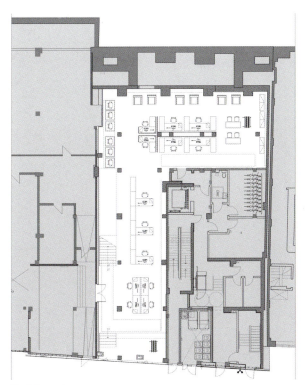

First-floor plan

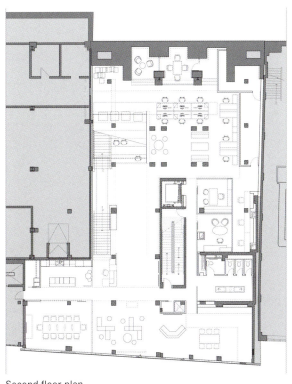

Second-floor plan

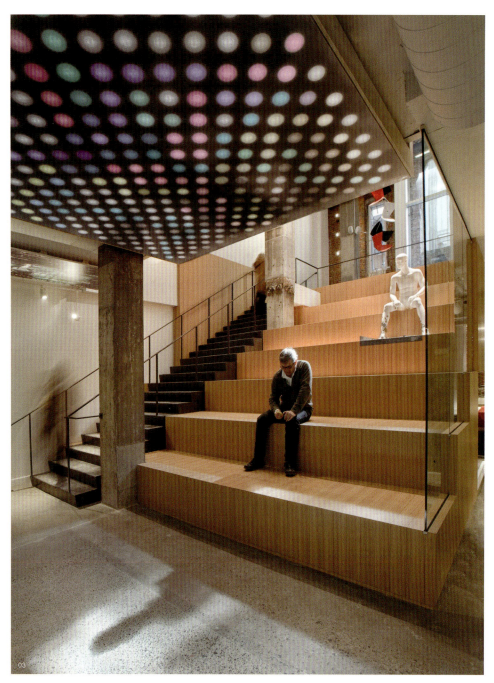

03 / Wooden stairs serving as meeting and
     display space
04 / Entrance guiding visitors through
     different zones
05 / Conference room
06 / Office

07 / Working area
08 / Display area
09 / Collaboration area

COR Shop

Location / Brasilia, Brazil
Area / 1938 square feet (180 square meters)
Completion / 2017
Design / BLOCO Arquitetos
Photography / Haruo Mikami

The shop is located in the underground parking of a shopping mall in Brasília, Brazil. The shop is a showroom for a Brazilian brand of paintings and architectural coatings and functions as the backdrop for displaying work of the furniture designer Paulo Alves. At the same time the space should be flexible enough to host parties and events.

Designers used colors to connect different functional areas in the interior and therefore transformed the abstract notion of color into something palpable in space. A series of white walls were created to serve mainly as a background for the furniture. These walls were positioned in space according to a single point of perspective at the main entrance of the shop. Therefore, from that specific point of view, the showroom looks like a sequence of white walls, floor, and ceiling. This specific point of observation is marked by a white circle on the floor inside the black room that precedes the entrance. However, small 'pockets' of colorful walls, floors, and ceilings are revealed as customers enter the shop. This was achieved following the lines of perspective from the defined point of view to define the limits of the color surfaces. The internal colors are only revealed through the movement of the visitor. A secondary display window faces a small group of parking spaces. Only from this point of view, it is possible to see the whole internal space at once.

01 / View from rear of store towards entrance

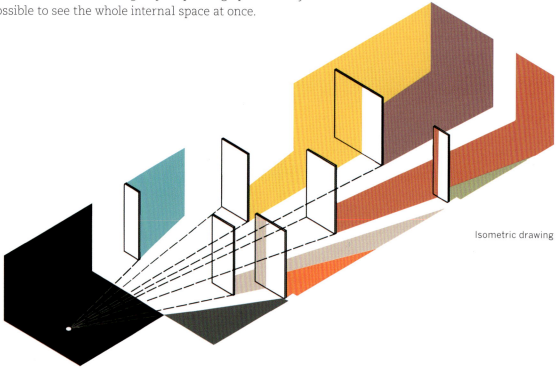

Isometric drawing

VERDITE

PAPOULA

VERMELHO
AMOR

POLEN

APA

CORTINA DE TEATRO

01

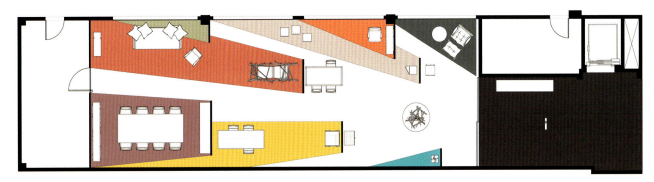
Plan

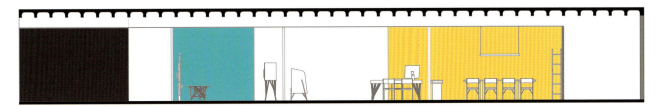
Section

05 / Pocket of color
06 / View of background

05

06

Fernando Jaeger Store—Pompeia

Location / São Paulo, Brazil
Area / 6512 square feet (605 square meters)
Completion / 2013
Design / SuperLimão Studio
Photography / Maíra Acayaba

The project was a new store of the Brazilian designer Fernando Jaeger, whose concepts have always pursued an accessible and timeless design that facilitates series production and also preserves the tradition of craft manufacturing techniques. He was one of the first professionals to use reforested wood in industrial furniture production and today works with different types of raw materials. At present, the stores sell an average of 2300 pieces per month and the designer is often invited to participate in national and international projects. The client wanted a retail space to attract customers' attention.

The client required that the building architecture should be kept as it was, and the jaboticaba (a typical Brazilian fruit) tree had to be kept. The conditions were accepted and the designer invited a studio to create the project for the store. The original structure was preserved and the restoration was done with additions for new elements. The outstanding characteristics of the place are wide windows, high ceilings, and a backyard with a view to the landscape. In order to give a nicer look, the walls of the house were just stripped and the original floor was kept. The whole space makes the customers feel comfortable. Walking and talking in this environment becomes a wonderful experience for them.

A charming touch was added by installing three big rollaway doors, integrating the interior with the big yard. Industrial modern elements, like electro-gutters, metal structured balconies, big iron gates, and a concrete floor, were added inside the house, making a combination in harmony with both the modern design and original elements.

01 / Interior of store

Plan

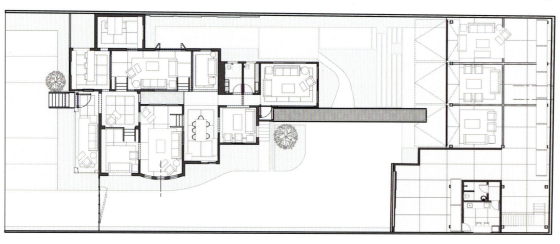

02 / Exterior of store
03 / Backyard
04 / Entrance showcasing products

Front elevation

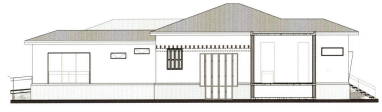

Left elevation

Back elevation

Right elevation

05 / Store interior organized in different floor levels

05

06

07

08

06 / Furniture display
07 / Stairs to lower level
08 / Preserved wood structure and stripped brick walls
09 / Backyard facing three big rollaway doors
10 / Displayed products

Section 1

Section 2

Fernando Jaeger Store—Moema

Location / São Paulo, Brazil
Area / 6458 square feet (600 square meters)
Completion / 2015
Design / SuperLimão Studio
Photography / Maíra Acayaba

This new store has three floors. The basement contains a parking lot and an area for technical loading and unloading. The first floor and upper floor houses the furniture products. The goal of the design was amplify the space of the large store and, at the same time, provide flexibility for the dynamics of the brand.

The idea of the façade emerges in order to work a prominent element made by Fernando Jaeger. The chair is organic. Observing this style, it can be noticed that it creates different volumes and distinct colors due to its shape. From this, designers did their own interpretation and turned it to the production, which made the pieces tailored to the project. These pieces create a set of light and shadow that makes the interior appear dynamic. In addition, at night, it shines artificial light into the street, highlighting the store and turning it into an urban lamp. From the entrance, customers can see all the depth of space, marked by the open plan and interrupted only by two small volumes of pinewood. The remaining space is geared for the exhibition of products that are disposed according to the modulation of the structure or exposed on shelves, also in pinewood and designed to this project.

Designers created a pergola in the rear area that enhances the depth of the shop and provides a transition between the interior and exterior created in the rear area, where a vertical planter brings the presence of vegetation into the store. The trusses and the pine ceiling mark the upper floor, and these elements combine with the created furniture to expose the products. The modulation of the metal structure is also utilized for the distribution of the electrical installations, serving as a basis for the lighting design.

01 / Storefront
02 / Interior of store

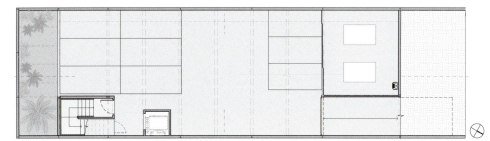

Second-floor plan

First-floor plan

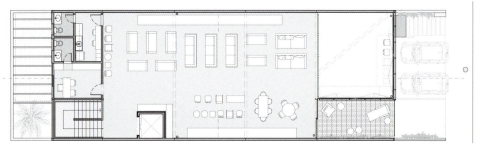

Basement plan

03 / Huge racks for display
04 / Display in entrance
05 / Products display

06 / Furniture display
07 / Connection between interior and exterior
08 / Furniture display in terrace
09 / Restroom

Cross section

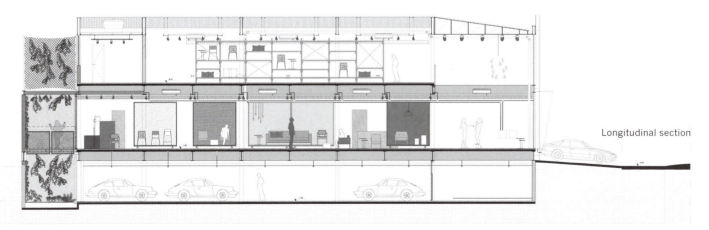

Longitudinal section

Lumini Rio

Location / Rio de Janeiro, Brazil
Area / 3358 square feet (312 square meters)
Completion / 2014
Design / studio mk27 (Marcio Kogan, Diana Radomysler, Luciana Antunes)
Photography / Reinaldo Cóser

The store was designed for selling light fixtures and lighting systems. Instead of taking the lamps out of context and placing them in a sterile space, the space creates environments for the products, as if in the consumer has entered a heartwarming domestic space. This was the main premise in designing the store.

The façade of the store is made with wooden muxarabi, a traditional element of Brazilian colonial and modern architecture. The material filters the external light and darkens the interior. Thus, customers in the showroom can see the effect of each fixture displayed, guaranteed by the glass façade and the visual transparency offered by the wooden lattice, all without losing any of the relationship to the outdoors. The wood also gives unity to the façade. Besides the large exhibition room, two closed and dark rooms make up the sales space. These rooms will display the light fixtures and special installations. Furthermore, an administrative office area with restricted access to the public was designed for employees.

The experience area in the store, composed of furniture created by classic and contemporary designers, can be used not only to give the products a display context, but also to provide the customers with the space for their experience, which can contribute to communication between the staff and customers. The customers can experience products in the comfortable space surrounded by lighting in the exhibition space. The store sought a feeling of coziness, which is one of the striking characteristics of the products. Thus, natural materials were used in the store. The strategy of creating different environments enhanced the versatility of the showroom as well, since the space can be rearranged with the arrival of new products. The store transports the comfort of home to the commercial space.

01 / Exterior of store
02 / Interior of store

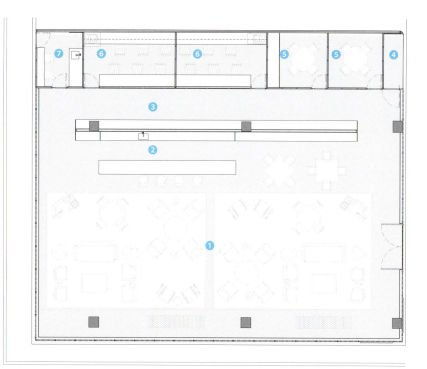

Plan

① Shop
② Bar
③ Corridor
④ Showcase
⑤ Effect room
⑥ Office
⑦ Kitchen

03 / Bar and exhibition corridor

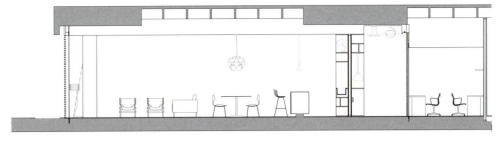

Cross section

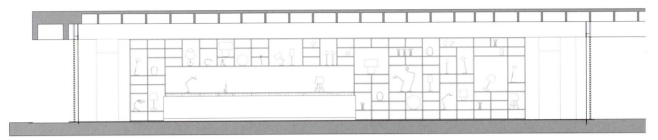

Longitudinal section

04–05 / Area for seating, meeting, and display
06 / Night view of store
07–08 / Furniture used for rest, meeting, and display

Drawing of front view

Drawing of side view

Normann Copenhagen Showroom

Location / Copenhagen, Denmark
Area / 18,299 square feet (1700 square meters)
Completion / 2016
Design / Normann Copenhagen
Photography / Normann Copenhagen

The new combined flagship store and showroom presents an exclusive and bold design concept that captures the essence of the brand. The style is raw and industrial, with a contrasting blend of materials. Epoxy, steel, reflective glass, and colored acrylic meet more organic elements, like plush rugs and shimmering terrazzo. The showroom is divided into four different zones: hall, stage, ballroom, and gallery. In the long foyer, a sofa stretches across the entire length of the hall. From rich golden hues on top of clear coral to deep wine-red, the sprawling sofa stands in a plush, warm contrast to the steel-clad hall.

The originality of Normann Copenhagen's new showroom is underscored by the store's second major exhibition 'Discovering Spaces.' The focus will be on textures and tactility when Normann Copenhagen opens the doors to its new exhibition. The store's characteristic long entrance way is filled with an undulating display of chairs from the Form furniture range. Various combinations of textiles and legs form an alluring multicolored furniture forest, transforming into a catalogue of inspirations for the more than 65,000 potential configurations that the customized chairs can offer. The exhibition forms a billowing passage, which encourages visitors to snake their way into the showroom. The largest wall in the showroom has been painted in colored stripes, with furls of soft, striped carpets growing outwards from its surface.

The third major design exhibition takes visitors along to a runway show with gold, glamorous, and unique show pieces. It is show time when Normann Copenhagen opens the doors to its new exhibition, the third of its kind in the unique concept showroom, which undergoes a complete metamorphosis every six months. In a remarkable transformation, the showroom's pillars and arches now open up to a completely naked room to make space for a spectacular installation. A dazzling sapphire yellow runway winds around the room.

01 / Striped walls clad with matching striped rugs for second showroom exhibition

Plan of second showroom exhibition

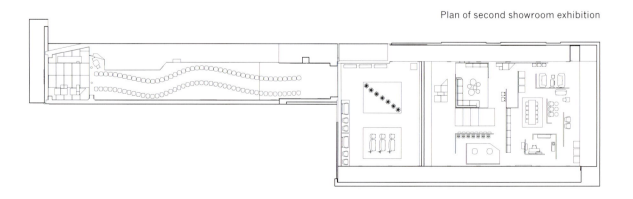

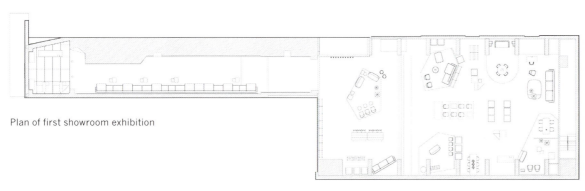

Plan of first showroom exhibition

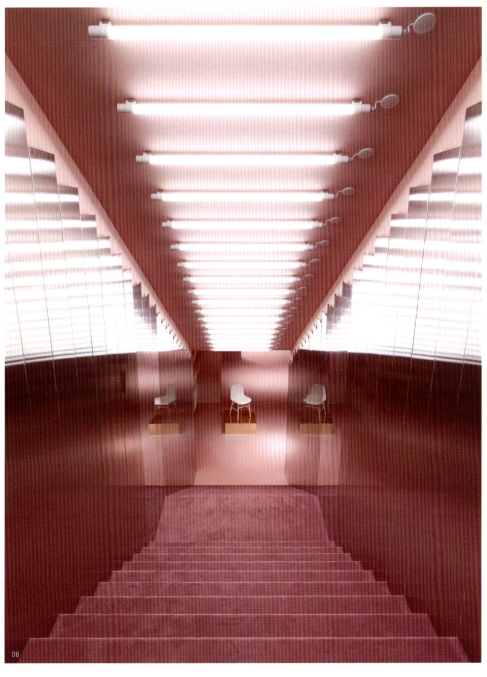

07 / Playful manipulation of visibility
08 / Many differently colored chairs in
     entrance hall
09 / Showroom filled with carefully
     curated displays
10 / Pouffe in gallery in shape of
     oversized mushroom
11 / Huge maze taking over old cinema
     auditorium

10

11

12 / Gallery transformed into cave
13 / Fashion world's runway shows as source of inspiration
14 / Runway theme with artistic backstage shots
15 / Chocolate-colored velvet sofa on runway
16 / Accessories and furniture stacked in showroom

Plan of third showroom exhibition

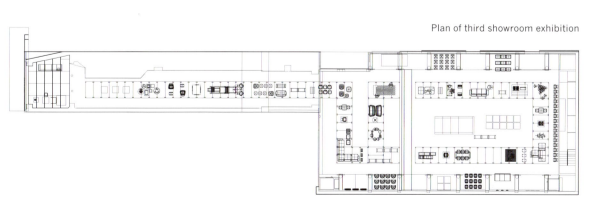

Olympia Tile &
Stone Retail Showroom

Location / Toronto, Canada
Area / 37,000 square feet (3437 square meters)
Completion / 2015
Design / II BY IV DESIGN
Photography / Hill Peppard Photography

As front-runners in the tile and stone industry, the brand Olympia Tile & Stone has great influence over styling and demand, particularly within not only North America, but also worldwide. Their flagship showroom occupies an entire block and spans 37,000 square feet (3437 square meters). Employing natural stone sourced from the client's product line, II BY IV DESIGN created a contemporary and stylish space with bold architectural feeling that references a gallery experience and high-end retail. The client's objectives for this project were direct: to create a new flagship store and become the largest and best designed full-service tile distributor in Toronto.

While the intent was to create the most spectacular showroom in the city, the renovation of the existing space posed many challenges. It was a constant challenge to determine where it made sense to allocate resources, ensuring the biggest impact on the customer experience without sacrificing or compromising the design intent. To create a strong graphical impact, black and white finishes were used throughout the showroom; matte black walls with white lacquered free-standing fixtures, contrasting black and white porcelain floors with a beautiful book-matched white marble cash desk and a black painted ceiling with repeating white light troughs. This black and white high contrast effect is classic, allowing the product to ultimately be the star. As a secondary benefit, it also creates a strong sense of space and acts as intuitive way-finding for consumers who may visit the expansive showroom for the first time.

Given the size of the space and the high-demand nature of the retailer, the decision was made to stay open during the renovations. Knowing this upfront, designers worked with the construction team to create a detailed schedule addressing each of the retailer's zones in a series of stages. The design team also worked closely with the client to identify areas that would have the biggest impact, and based on the area's importance to the customer's experience, assigned a dollar value for what was to be spent relevant to the project's success. With this strategy, the design team was able to creatively and practically carry out their creative vision.

01 / Interior of showroom
02 / Custom benches

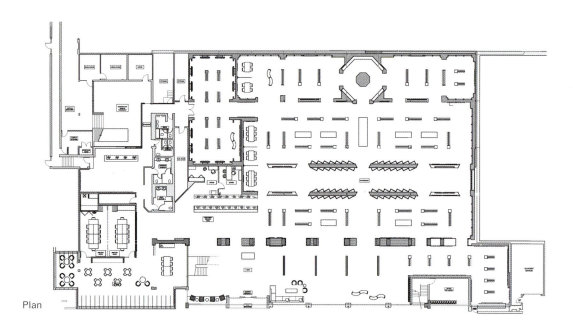

Plan

03

04 / Details of cash desk
05 / Cash desk
06 / Natural mosaics

TOG Flagship Store

Location / São Paulo, Brazil
Area / 22,690 square feet (2108 square meters)
Completion / 2015
Design / TRIPTYQUE
Photography / Ricardo Bassetti

Conceived as a multipurpose space, the flagship store will also function as a major social hub with the ambition of stirring up the concept of selling design. The space looks like a machine with variable geometry adapting to different usages.

There are parts that look quite industrial and parts that look quite homely, with plants, rugs, and mismatched chairs. That contrast is required to allow the different functions to be installed in this repository. The container was neutralized, becoming absent in the visuals, thanks to an immaculate white. The plants were already there, reminding people they are in a tropical megalopolis where nature is a part of the urban space. In order to be simple but economic, designers used an existing space with some readymade features.

Roughness of the existing walls and brand-new flooring creates contrast. The lights are suspended from the concrete beams visible on the ceiling. The project was conceived to allow the organic spaces to change over time. The lack of walls between sections, an electrical system that pervades the entire area, and the application of materials like glass facilitates multiple uses for the space.

01 / Exterior of store
02 / Interior of store

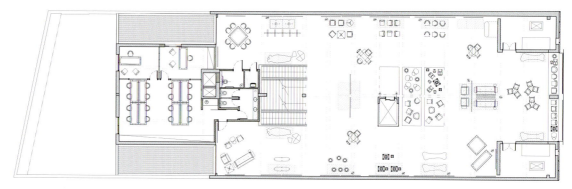

Second-floor plan

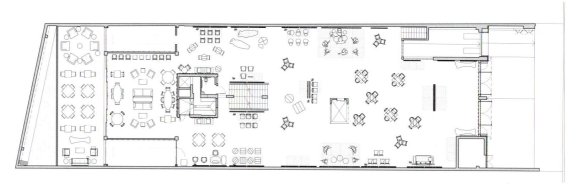

First-floor plan

04

05

03 / Staircase connecting two floors
04–05 / Colorful decorations and furniture
in white space

157

Xtra's Herman Miller Shop-in-shop

Location / Singapore
Area / 9063 square feet (842 square meters)
Completion / 2016
Design / PRODUCE WORKSHOP PTE LTD
Photography / PRODUCE WORKSHOP, XTRA
DESIGNS, Edward Hendricks, CI&A Photography

This new flagship store is located at the Marina Square in Singapore. The continuous surface-like canvas stretches across the entire site, leading the viewers from the low entrance to a high glass curtain wall. The structure is made of plywood, and features a new plywood construction technique adapted from tailoring.

Being an established multi-brand furniture retailer in Singapore, the idea of a shop-in-shop was a response to Xtra's desire to showcase a comprehensive range of Herman Miller products in a space. To reflect the image of the brand, the lightness and warmth of the plywood material and technological innovations of the work chairs have been combined. Having learned from key products and their design processes, the solution seeks to develop a soft and porous 'skin' for the store. Originally used for shaping fabric to fit the human body, the designers used this technique onto plywood. The darts and their respective angles on a flat piece of plywood determine the eventual curvature when closed. Circular cut-outs are used at the converging point of the darts to allow the plywood to bend and avoid tears. When assembled, the structure forms a naturally undulated surface much like the stretching of fabric.

The most challenging part of the project was the translation from flat pattern drawing to three-dimensional modeling. A combination of computer simulation and physical modeling helped to achieve the desired curvature. The elasticity of the plywood played a major factor in the shaping of the skin, and the dart angles had to be recalibrated to accommodate any changes in the type of the plywood material. Compared with conventional design and construction techniques, this component-based design process demands greater continuity and simultaneous planning across all stages of the project. This fabric wood structure pushes the boundaries of plywood construction.

01 / Main entrance
02 / Interior of store

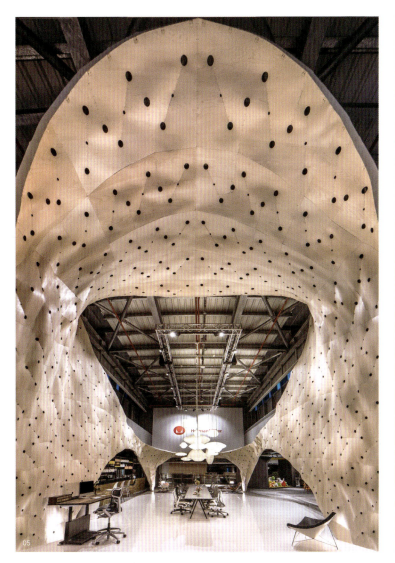

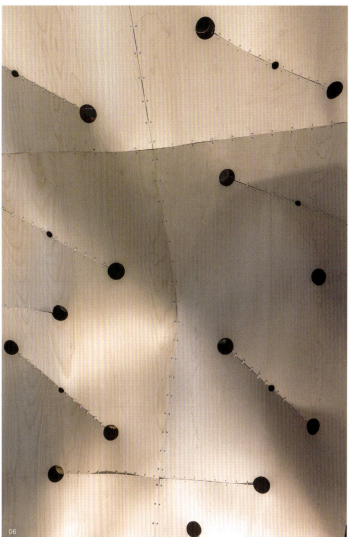

03 / Fabric wood as tensile plywood system
04 / Area connecting showroom and café
05 / Tall arch
06 / Details of fabric wood used for connection

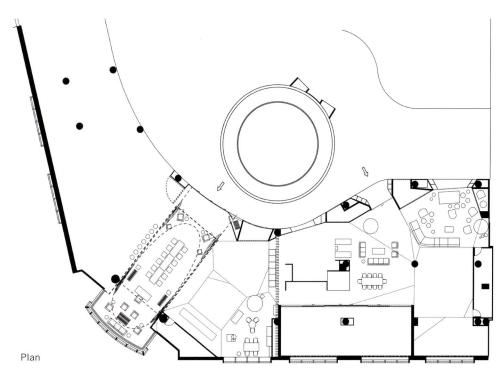

Plan

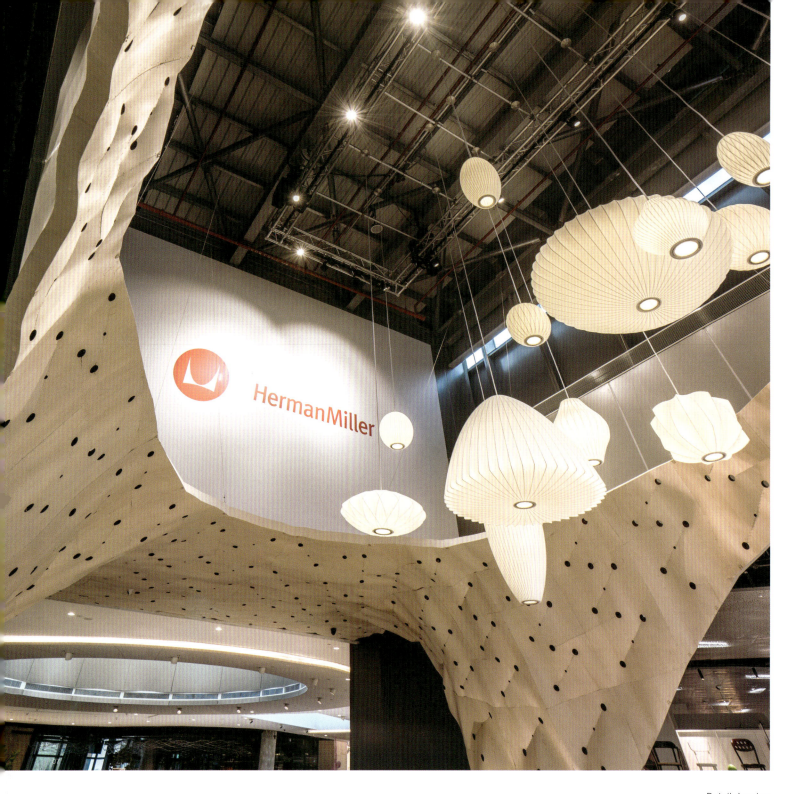

Detail drawing

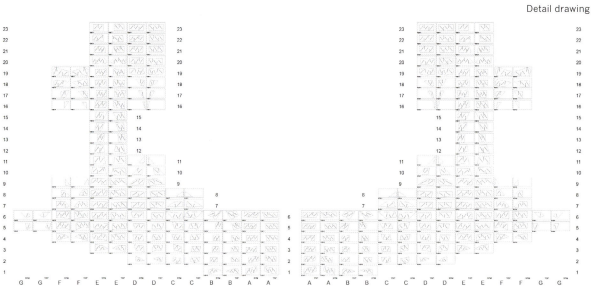

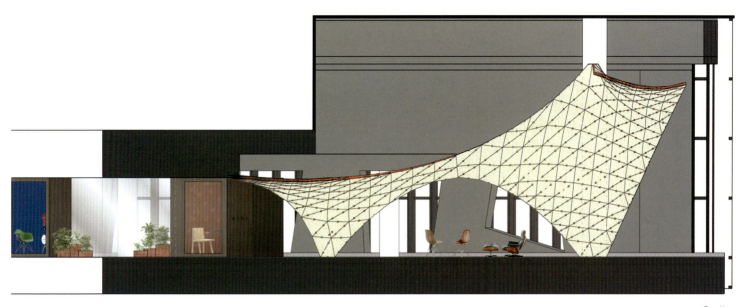

Section

07 / Herman Miller's iconic logo on wall
08 / Natural undulation of fabric wood

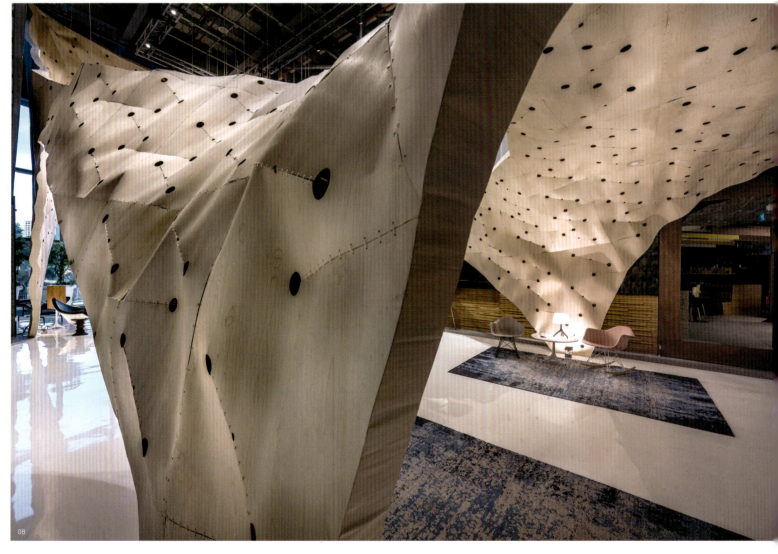

08

Life Story

Location / Tokyo, Japan
Area / 1076 square feet (100 square meters)
Completion / 2015
Design / AXIS Inc. (Eiji Yoshida, Yuichi Minagawa),
id inc. (Seiji Oguri, Yohei Oki)
Photography / shuntaro (bird and insect ltd.)

The store was designed for Sony to display products for its new concept 'Life Space UX.' The concept is that products themselves do not stand out, but blend into the space, creating a new experience for customers through image and sound.

To realize that concept, interior space was colored white, symbolizing basic background of daily life. Floor, walls, and ceiling were seamlessly connected so that living place and people become closer and free. The space had an impressive design expressing the concept, and also let customers enter and walk in the store easily and freely. Customers can go in and out the store from anywhere. This was paired with the concept 'Life Space UX,' which allows customers can use the products from anywhere. Regarding façade, pattern of exterior tiles were put on a large window to block direct sunlight and keep store luminosity appropriate. Vertical blinds instead of curtains were installed on the window in order to keep living and theater space dimmer, which also helped creating a cool space.

In order to clarify characteristics of each room in the store, the important thing was placing furniture and miscellaneous goods rather than making special treatment or reformation for floor, wall, and ceiling. Such an arrangement fit with the design concept, in which image and sound can change the space. This is a place with a big challenge to realize both maximum expression for products and minimum decoration in the store, since the store had to open only in a few weeks.

01 / Façade
02 / View from living and theater space

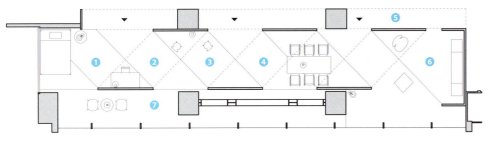

Plan

① Bed space
② Study
③ Children's space
④ Dining space
⑤ Kitchen
⑥ Living and theater space
⑦ Garden

03 / View from bed space
04 / View from living and theater space
05 / Dining space

03

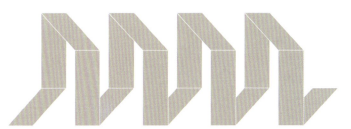

Diagram (space)

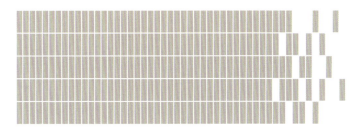

Diagram (window)

VONNA

Location / Madrid, Spain
Area / 2583 square feet (240 square meters)
Completion / 2016
Design / PYO arquitectos (Paul Galindo Pastre, Ophélie Herranz Lespagnol)
Photography / Imagen Subliminal / Miguel de Guzman, Rocio Romero

This project is a transformation of an old store into a kitchen showroom in center of Madrid. The project is built with distances: distances with the existing, distances between materials, distances between spaces, distances between objects, and distances between times. The designers and client aim at providing a better experience for customers in this store.

The new separates from the old. Thus, the shop window carpentry is attached to the façade anchoring from the outside, presenting the existing structure, appropriating its qualities, yet detaching itself from it. The execution, assembly, and detail are a presentation of the interior intervention. The carpentry is folded to distance itself from the street and welcome the client in a 'domestic' space. Its delicate materiality steps away from the bare space that surrounds it and from the movement of the street. The marble that defines the interior showcase plinth leans out of the street and invites people to enter. The intervention on existing materials is focused on recovering their 'gross' qualities. The terrazzo tiles are diamond polished. The suspended ceilings are dismantled and the building concrete skeleton appears. The surfaces are undressed revealing their folds, their superimposed accidents, allowing a glimpse of excavated time.

In the main space, new materials connect existing ones through joining elements, like brass profiles in the marble cuttings, wood strips in the partitions supports, and metal anchors in the pine wood uprights of the exhibition wall. The project juxtaposes in the same space two contrasting themes, revealing the space between them: a temporary space where fragments acquire a certain thickness, and architecture built from the experience accumulated the remains of older buildings.

01 / Façade
02 / Shop window

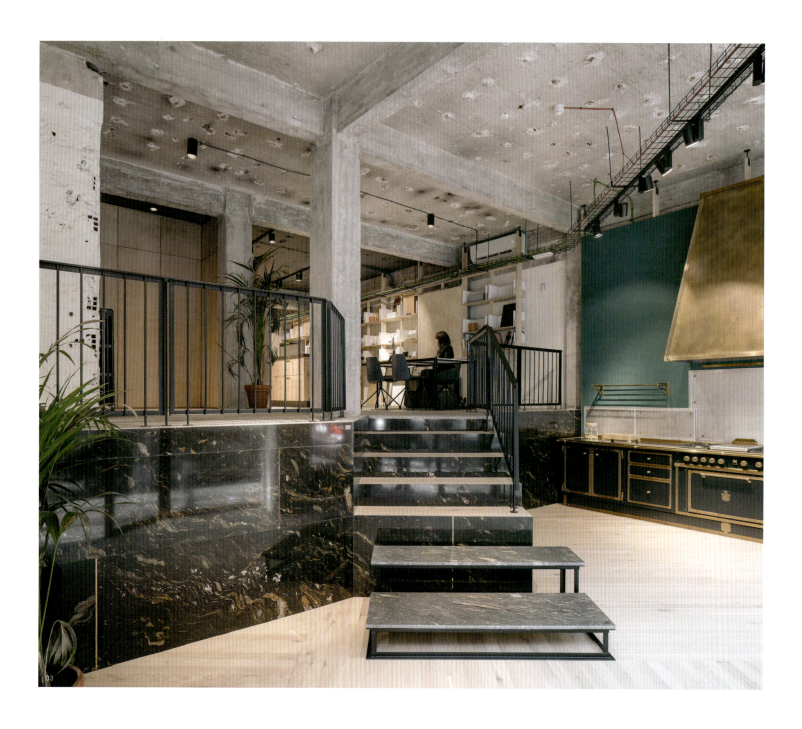

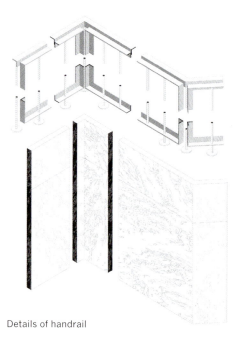

Details of handrail

Axonometric drawing
of shop window

Axonometric drawing
of kitchen showroom

03 / Stairs to main space
04 / Main space
05 / Working area

Arda Showroom

Location / Zhejiang, China
Area / 10,764 square feet (1000 square meters)
Completion / 2017
Design / LUKSTUDIO
Photography / Peter Dixie for LOTAN Architectural
Photography, PROJECT|ION| motion picture production

Based on the idea that a kitchen is the heart of a home, the designers created a culinary 'village' where kitchen appliances are displayed in four domestic settings, alongside a gallery, a cooking classroom, a VIP lounge, and a multifunctional courtyard. The design has transformed the original space into a complete brand experience.

A white box marks the entrance of the journey. Following stepping stones in the shallow water, people enter a dark tunnel. An introductory video on the left is accompanied by a water feature of dishwasher jets. The main display area is organized as a series of white huts, each presenting an ideal kitchen, ranging from minimalistic white, total black, rustic country, and modern American. Designers have placed these volumes carefully, carving out strategic openings to create a visual dialogue with one's movement.

Walking along the stone pavement, a vaulted shed stands out within the quiet 'village.' Reminiscent of an outdoor kiln, the space displays the evolution of oven technology and creates an interesting twist in the spatial experience. Next to the red-brick structure, a fully-equipped classroom with movable doors and cooking stations provide a multifunctional area for try-out sessions and company events. Passing windows with views to the exterior courtyard, people reach the VIP lounge where exquisite dinners are served. Lined with travertine stone slabs and walnut wood panels, this elegant room promises memorable gatherings. To top it all, people are welcomed into the adjacent conservatory and outdoor courtyard where herbs are planted and picked to garnish their dishes. Reinventing the experience of a conventional kitchen showroom, designers created an artificial village of different homes, set in a cozy courtyard that brings water, daylight and plants into close proximity. The project presents consumers' experience and also reflects on the essence of an ideal living environment.

01 / View towards showroom

Model diagrams

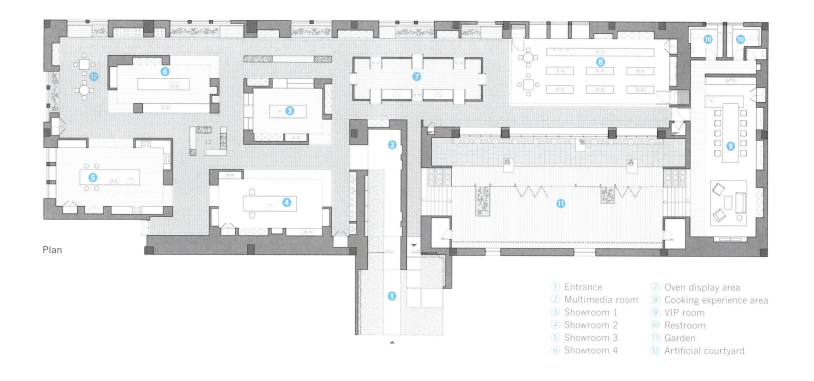

Plan

1. Entrance
2. Multimedia room
3. Showroom 1
4. Showroom 2
5. Showroom 3
6. Showroom 4
7. Oven display area
8. Cooking experience area
9. VIP room
10. Restroom
11. Garden
12. Artificial courtyard

02 / Showroom

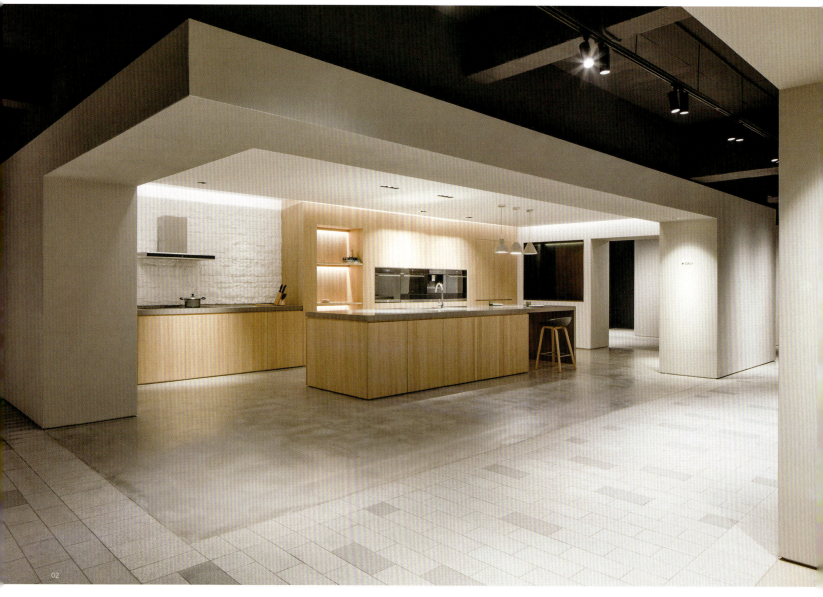

03–04 / Interior of showroom

05 / Artificial courtyard
06 / View towards showroom

07 / Passage in showroom

Model diagram

Rational Exhibition Hall

Location / Fujian, China
Area / 3229 square feet (300 square meters)
Completion / 2017
Design / DC. Design (Lin Kaixin)
Photography / Wu Yongchang

The Rational cabinets originated in Germany and the new showroom was located in Fuzhou of Fujian Province, China. The designer integrated the western elements into the Chinese store, insisting on the use of western industrial technology and integration of Chinese characteristics and exploring the requirements of modern spiritual life.

01 / Entrance
02 / Interior of store

The concept of the design is renovation and mystery. Maintaining the original architecture, the designer found a new path. Abandoning the entire curtain wall made of glass, the use of black-gray aluminum grille and simple external wall enclose the store. Taking German craftsmanship advocating precision as the starting point, the designer created the entrance as a beveled box. Black and gray bring the strong sense of ritual. The waterscape on the left of the entrance acts as landscape optimization and isolation zone. The independent two floors were got through, creating the sense of layer because of narrow entrance and spacious interior. Getting through the two floors made the structural beam visible. To make up the disadvantage, the designer adopted the mirror design to turn its original architectural disadvantage into flash point.

The display shelves are extended from the second floor to the first floor, enriching the visual experience. The warm colors narrow the distance between people and space. Irregular vessels are placed on the display shelves, conveying people's attitude towards life and presenting comfortable lifestyle. The second floor includes the tea taste area and experience area. Kitchen is no longer a single functional area for cooking, but a multi-functional area for communication among people. Light is an important element in design. Natural light penetrate into the tea taste area through the grille, creating the hazy beauty and making people focus on the displayed products. The south wall of the enclosed wall was carefully arranged with an opening, which is the only window overlooking the outside world. People can chat in the salon area.

01

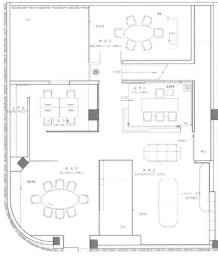

Second-floor plan

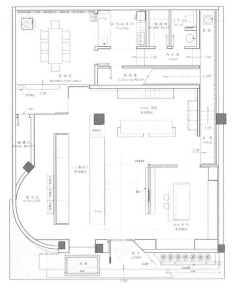

First-floor plan

03 / Passage
04 / Display rack extending from second to first floor
05 / Wooden table and chairs
06 / Planform

Vigor Space

Location / Jiangsu, China
Area / 12,917 square feet (1200 square meters)
Completion / 2017
Design / NONEZONE Space Atelier
Photography / Chen Ming

The project is a brand-new retail store located in a shopping mall. The store places emphasis on the improvement of the offline consumption and customer experience. Besides the sales of fresh retail items, there is coffee, ice cream, flowers, wine, and other products. In addition, dining and gathering spaces were also added, providing a comprehensive range of functions. The main side faces the outdoor atrium.

Designers wanted customers enter the wine store with a sense of curiosity. The interior furnishings are openly displayed in order to reduce visual barriers and add rhythm with the combination of dynamic and static pieces.

Considering the diversity of products, light-grey terrazzo and wood are the primary colors for the space, which makes harmony with colorful articles. A large space is set at the end of the store, which can be used for lectures, parties, and salons.

01 / Stepped cabinet for both storage and display

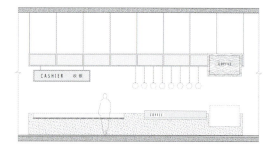

Elevation 1

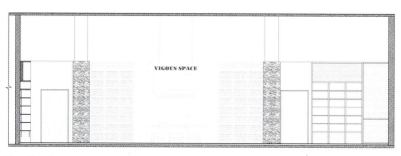

Elevation 2

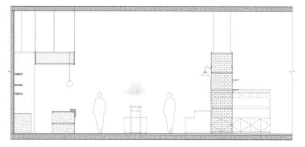

Elevation 3

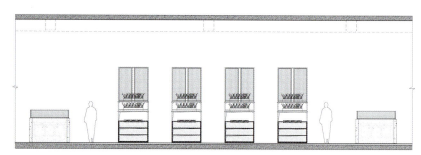

Elevation 4

Plan

1. Reception desk
2. Café
3. Flowers area
4. Furnishing area
5. Children's activity area
6. Import commodity area
7. Non-staple food area
8. Wine area
9. Kitchen
10. Seafood area
11. Western cuisine area
12. Japanese cuisine area
13. Salon

02 / View towards import commodity area from wine area
03 / Passage for visual extension
04 / Primary and secondary passage at entrance

05 / Resting area
06 / Display cabinet around resting area
07 / Fresh food display and processing area
08 / Japanese cuisine area

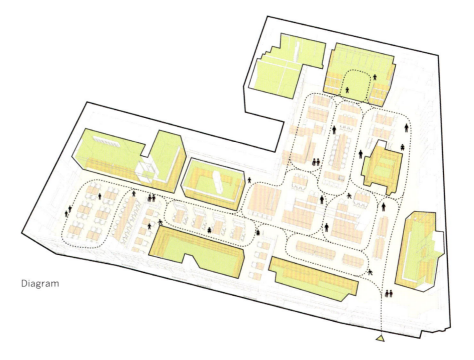

Diagram

Bazar Noir

Location / Berlin, Germany
Area / 915 square feet (85 square meters)
Completion / 2014
Design / Hidden Fortress
Photography / Hidden Fortress

The store opened its doors to the public to showcase its selections of hand-picked objects and interior accessories. In order to allow for a constant change of exhibits, the task was to design an extremely adaptable and flexible space, preferably leaving the atmosphere of the raw building and the lofty character of the space intact.

Black is the anchor in the concept work for the store. The special presentation of the second floor was achieved by separating it in a stark contrast from the rest of the store. Using maritime pine as a main component provides a strong image due to its large grain, in its original light white or yellowish color as well as in tinted black. While it became the main material for the upper floor in its original color, it was also used in black for most of the furniture of the main floor. Thus the upper floor with its strongly different atmosphere could at the same time be integrated and separated from the darker main floor. Elements of copper, glass, and high-quality fabrics were added, resulting in an overall warm and cozy atmosphere in spite of the minimalism of the store interior.

The dominating areas and visual axis's of the main floor are the tea kitchen in the back part of the room and the presentation rack in the front, a glass-top counter, the side walls of the staircase, and a glass wall at the front edge of the balcony. The divisions and connections between these areas are designed to allow a variety of new perspectives. This softens the division between the upper and lower area, and contradicts the stronger division of dark downstairs and light upstairs. Due to an optimized use of the available space, the tea kitchen was integrated into the interior. The kitchen therefore provides comfort and function to customers and the staff. Designers had to handle daylight from three different spots and thus worked with an extra-matte wall paint, which absorbs most of the existing light to set up light spots precisely. In the front room, a rack of spotlights is placed under the high ceiling.

01 / Floating staircase in store
02 / Black as central color for store

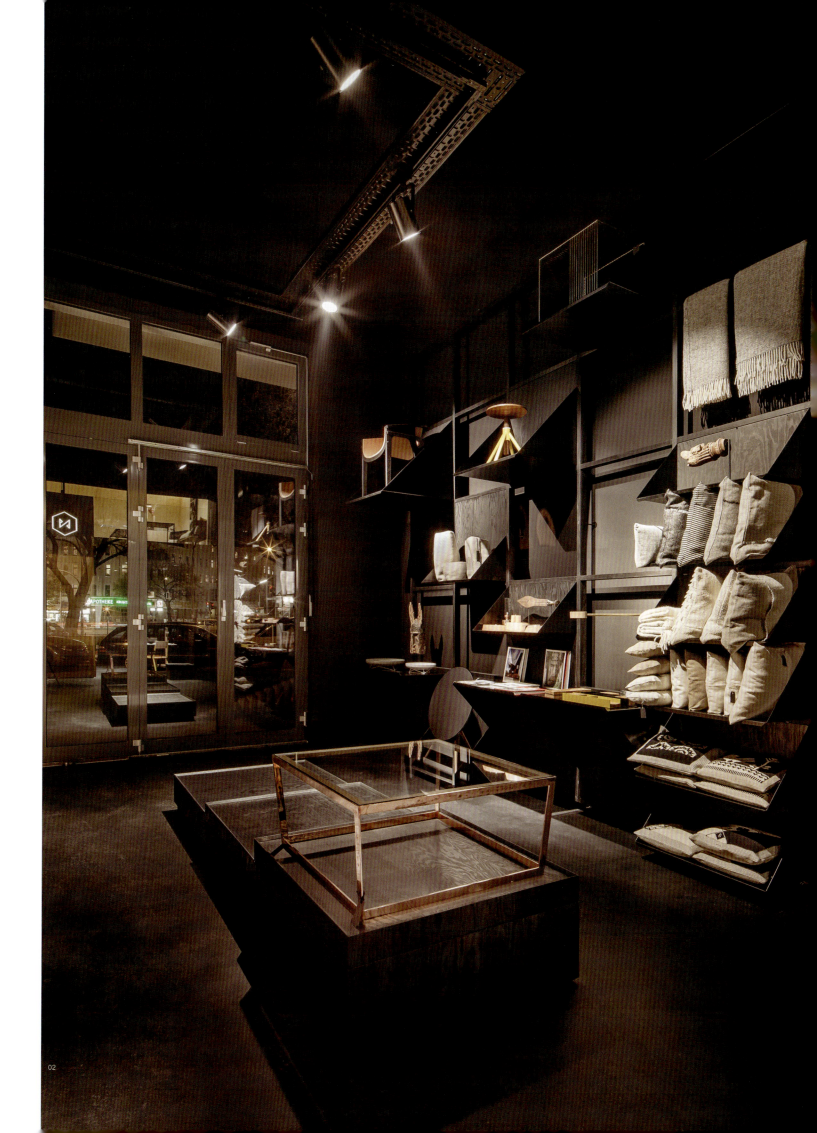

Mezzanine plan

First-floor plan

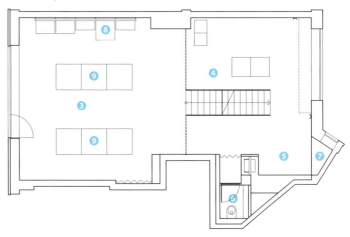

1 Mezzanine
2 Storage
3 Sales room 1
4 Sales room 2
5 Kitchen
6 Restroom
7 Light shaft
8 Shelf system
9 Flexible shop system

03 / Customized and adjustable shelf system
04 / Silhouette of staircase defining room underneath mezzanine
05 / Main room and central staircase

03

06 / Sink used from both sides
07 / Top of staircase in center of mezzanine
08 / Pine wood and surrounding light strip

Modifiable shelf system for displaying items

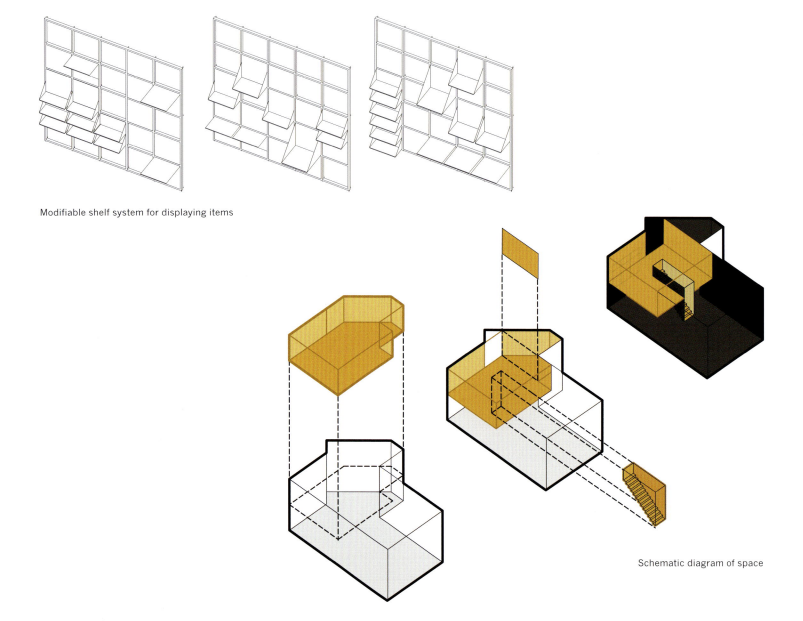

Schematic diagram of space

07

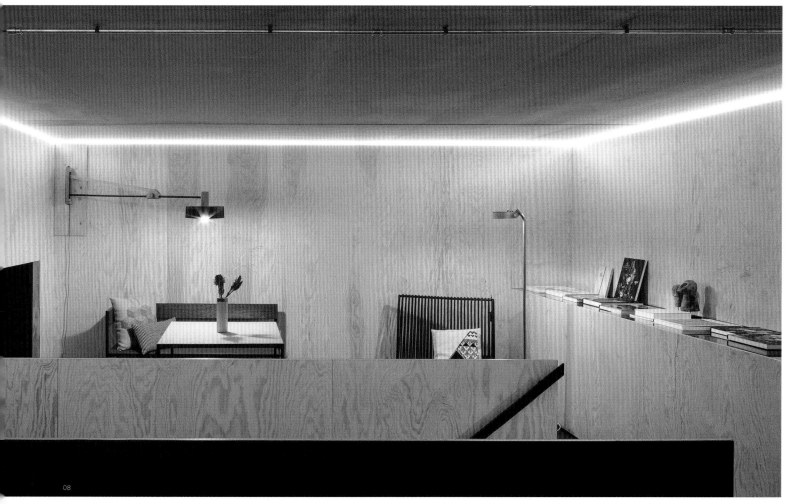

08

Groos Concept Store

Location / Rotterdam, The Netherlands
Area / 3229 square feet (300 square meters)
Completion / 2017
Design / MVRDV
Photography / Ossip van Duivenbode

01 / Interior of store

The store set out to fill a gap between designer and consumer and to create a space where a selection of great products could be displayed and bought. The idea was an innovative store showcasing a cutting-edge selection of what Rotterdam has to offer in terms of art and design. The store is located in an urban area where growing tech start-ups, creative entrepreneurs, and artists can meet to eat, shop, and relax.

In The Wall Street Journal, Elle, Architectural Digest, and even The Lonely Planet, the store has been named as a leading example for promoting leading trends in the world of design, art, food, and culture in Rotterdam. The store has also started heading in a different direction, focusing more on a range of high-end artistic collaborations while staying true to its original concept: promoting local talent from Rotterdam to a wider audience. The store's distinct bright pink wall displays original artwork.

The design proposal restores the space to its original form and makes the shop compact by creating a custom-built cabinet of Rotterdam products, providing maximum floor space for changing events and gallery programs. Its original function as a communal building is now being restored, returning it to its former glory.

First-floor plan

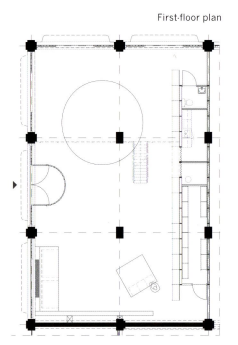

Second-floor plan

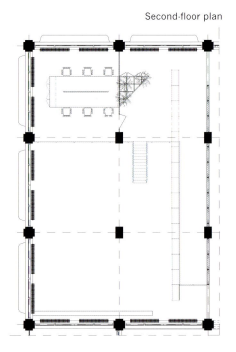

01

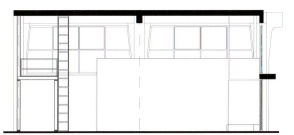

Cross section

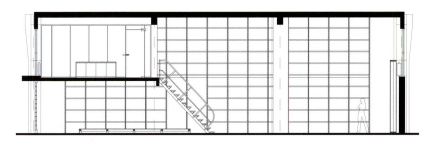

Longitudinal section

02 / Interior space divided into two floors
03 / Pink wall displaying artworks and
mint green counter
04 / Circular display table
05 / Space for rotating events and gallery
program

04

05

ROOM Concept Store

Location / Bangkok, Thailand
Area / 1722 square feet (160 square meters)
Completion / 2016
Design / Maincourse Architect Co., Ltd.
Photography / Ketsiree Wongwan

The store is an exclusive lifestyle multi-brand store, letting customers indulge themselves in a collection of furniture, decoration, stationery and artworks. The store is located in a renovated space with limited width and height. Physical challenge of the site is to circulate traffic efficiently within the low-ceiling elongated site. The multi-level platforms are designed to create a new exciting experience to the customers.

By dividing the space into three main corridors lengthwise and connecting them sporadically through openings in between, this creates a large space in the center where customers can move around. The central space is then elevated to create multi-level platforms that showcase products and double as circulation links between the main corridors. The platforms take shape in the form of 'tables' that customers can step on, offering a unique experience of moving not only horizontally, but also vertically. This allows customers to have different angles to view the products. Polycarbonate shelves are used to define the corridors. Besides displaying products, the translucency and transparency of the shelves give the visual connection between the outside and the inside. Changeable polycarbonate sheets can be rearranged to emphasize certain products and create a fresh look. Therefore, it results in a modular system that articulates each polycarbonate sheet together using only uniquely designed teakwood joint made by local craftsmen to hold polycarbonate sheets into sturdy shelves, with the help of metal rods inserted perfectly into gaps between sheet's structures to reinforce the shelves. This results in design integrating craftsmanship techniques with industrial material.

In conclusion the point of the design was to create an engaging environment for customers of various ages to not just enjoy choosing products but also creating a fun and exciting environment for children to run around the store's corridor-like paths. This design direction will encourage both children and adults to explore the furniture and the spaces created, giving a new shopping experience with each visit.

01 / Adjustable shelves for variable products' size

Drawings of retail space

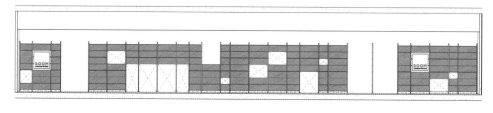

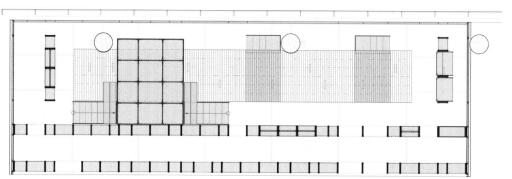

02 / Shelf's opening creating perfect angle for specific products
03 / Multi-leveled presentation
04 / Polycarbonate sheet and teak joints blending industrial craftsmanship

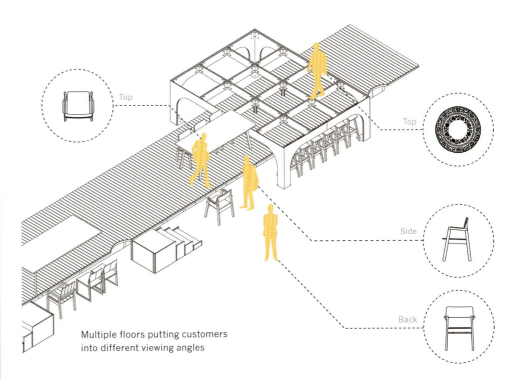

Top

Top

Side

Back

Multiple floors putting customers into different viewing angles

04

05 / Upper level provides overview angle
06 / Multi-level space delivering presentation space
     for products
07 / Connected corridors offering continuous
     experience for customers

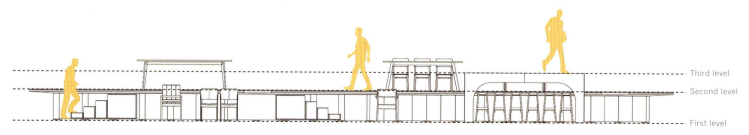

Third level

Second level

First level

Table tops acting as floor for other tables

Kki Sweets and the Little Dröm Store

Location / Singapore
Area / square feet (square meters)
Completion / 2015
Design / PRODUCE WORKSHOP PTE LTD
Photography / Edward Hendricks, CI&A Photography

The Little Dröm Store offers knick-knacks driven by art and design, and Kki Sweets sells beautifully handcrafted Japanese-inspired French mousse. They share a space at the School of the Arts in Singapore.

While the two brands share a storefront, they need to retain their distinctive identities, yet not look like two completely separate entities. The datum plane within the shop is designed as a porous trellis so that the entire diagram can be observed and experienced from within. In the Kki Sweets section, volumes above the plane hints at the imaginary, while the volumes below are adapted to practical requirements of experiencing and merchandising, forming tables and shelves, intimate interiors, and close-knit exteriors. The plane continues into the store inversely. Instead of forming voids, it occupies a volume that forms the floor of a 'tree house' (a theme closely related to the brand).

With the idea of the datum plane linking the two shops at a higher level, the shops are actually considered as separate and independent entities on the ground. They are seen as occupying an open space, separated by an 'internal street' leading in from the main door with their frontage and signage orientated toward each other. This street-like space extends into Kki, meandering between the volumes of rooms. The primary materials used are maple veneered plywood for the volumes and solid pine strips for the trellis. They are selected for their light color so that the structure acts like a blank canvas on which the two shops can be filled with colors with their variety of products. The light-colored maple and pine also help contrast with the darker colors of the atrium. Despite the visual lightness the timber volumes convey, there is actually a hollow steel framework within. Supports to the ground are disguised as table legs and door frames to achieve a lifted effect.

01 / Interior of store

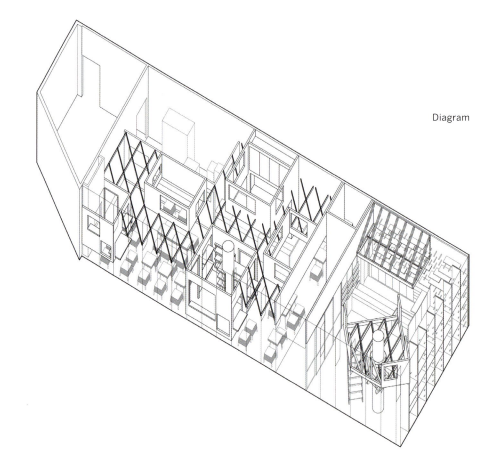

Diagram

Section

M.Y.Lab Wood Workshop

Location / Shanghai, China
Area / 4844 square feet (450 square meters)
Completion / 2017
Design / Continuation Studio
Photography / SHIROMIO Studio

The workshop is located on the first floor of a warehouse in Shanghai. The center teaches and showcases Wood crafting, packaging this traditional technique as a rediscovered treasure.

This design proposed an implementing an 'archaeological excavation site' into the original space. The main wood crafting room is forged into a secluded space, positioned on the sunken floor behind the entrance wall, enclosed by a low wall made of terrazzo. Above this space lays a massive pent roof, formed by a black metal mesh. The staircase attached to the entrance wall leads to the corridor on the first floor, where visitors can lean against the fences and the wood crafting operations are on display. Visitors can also work on their projects, or simply do some reading or have a chat while using the crafting tables by the window. A narrow and lofty corridor is set as the entrance to the main space. A series of display cabinets and LED screens are installed continuously on the wooden wall. Meanwhile, a space under the screen closest to the entrance is designed for exhibiting furniture works. Utilizing the triangle space formed by the slopping ceiling of the main space, a two-step terrace is designed into the classroom on the second floor, increasing its internal area.

In addition, two black metal 'boxes' are introduced into the route. One, with a staircase inside, is located between the two storys as a transportation junction, whose tilted top parallels the form of the ceiling in the main space. The other, functioning as the tearoom, is located between the attached room and its yard as a pathway, for rest. In order to enhance the visual sensation of floating of the second story, the load-bearing structures design for the added interlayer has become significant. The solution is to lift up the primary beams of the second floor with only five columns.

1 Slanting roof
2 Light box
3 Flexible classroom
4 Black box (staircase)
5 Sunken space (crafting room)
6 Wooden structure
7 Black box (tea room)

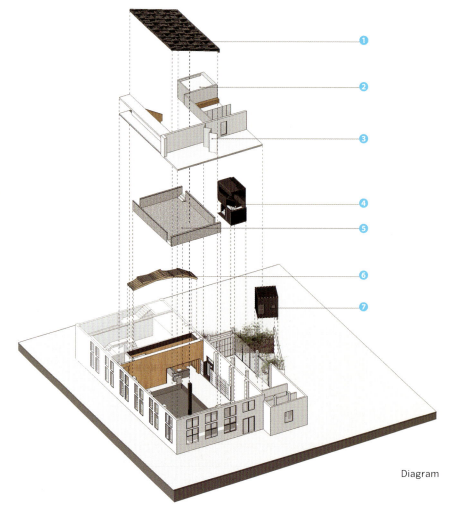

Diagram

01 / View overlooking 'archaeological
excavation site'
02 / Entrance

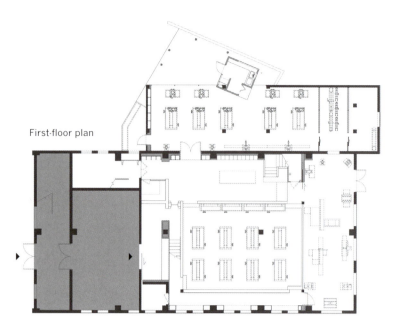

First-floor plan

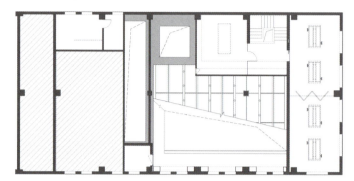

Second-floor plan

03

05 / Reception under wooden arch structure
06 / Heavy machinery room next to 'archaeological excavation site'
07 / Staircase connecting floors

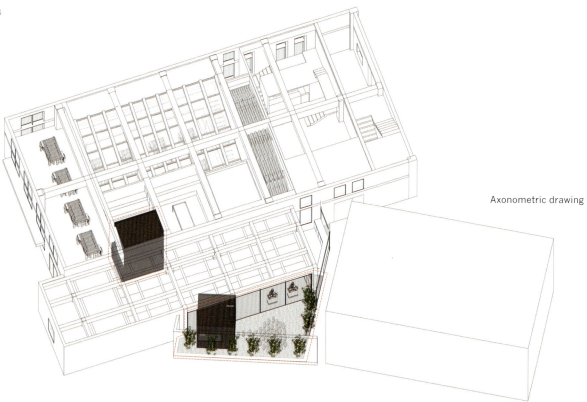

Axonometric drawing

The Inverted Truss

Location / Taipei, Taiwan, China
Area / 7911 square feet (735 square meters)
Completion / 2016
Design / B+P Architects, dotze innovations studio
Photography / Hey! Cheese, Wei Tze-Chun, Lin Tzu-Li

The store was renovated from a historic house used to sell rice. There are three floors in the store. The designers used the first floor for selling rice. The second floor was designed as a creative cultural space. The third floor consists of an office and a display room of cultural relics.

01 / Staircase in interior

Given this historic building to work with, the designers discussed how to integrate the new modern structure into the old historic building. The designers retained existing materials and structural forms, attempting to make balance between new and old levels. The designers regarded the structure as furniture, using the self-supporting and wooden inverted trusses to support the roof truss and integrating the lighting and equipment pipelines, transforming the structure into a single object. In addition to the basic repair of the entire building, the designers attempted to reuse a small number of dismantled materials with minor adjustments. The main design was based on the principle that the historic building should be properly preserved, and damage should be reduced to a minimum.

In addition, many rice millers had originally existed along the street. The renovation of the space was to recover the rice shop atmosphere of the area, letting the woodwork act as a historic relic describe the space. This texture can be regarded as a kind of respect for the old building.

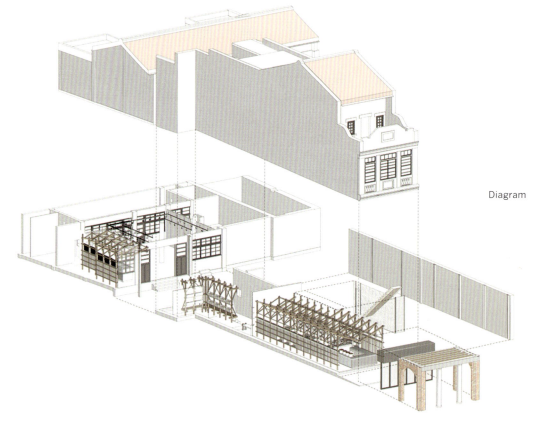

Diagram

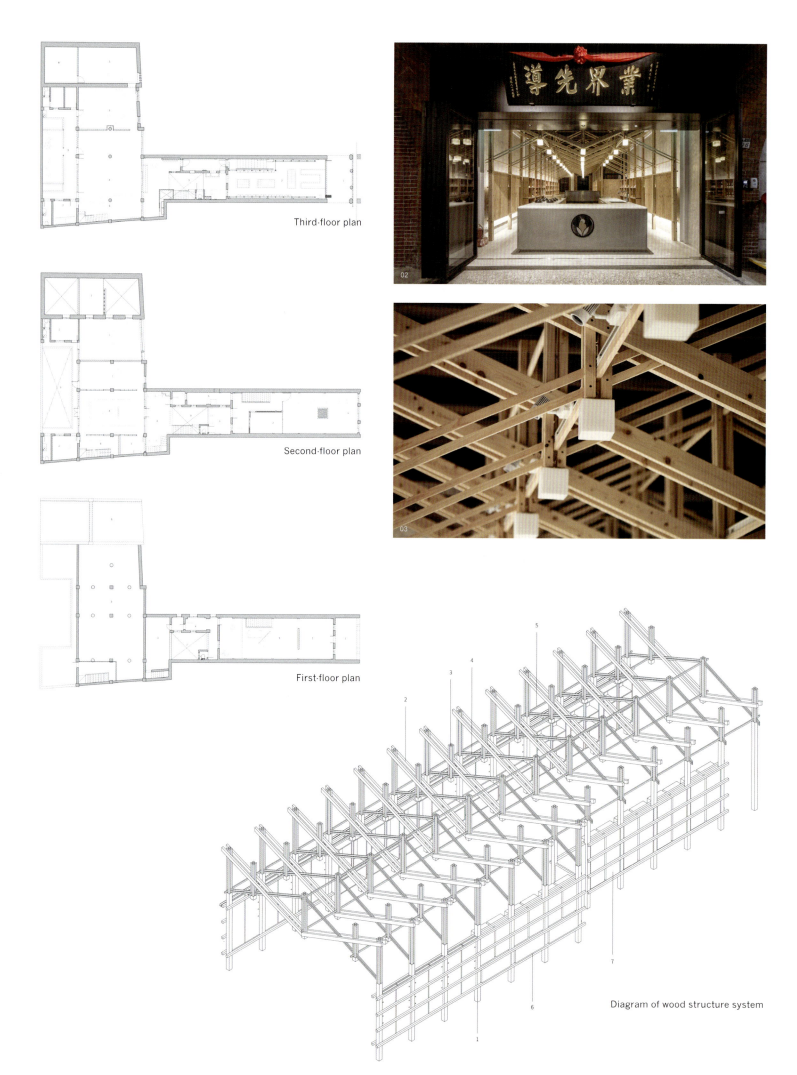

Third-floor plan

Second-floor plan

First-floor plan

Diagram of wood structure system

02 / New appearance of historic building
03 / Integration of structure and light system
04 / Interior of store
05 / New inverted trusses and old structure

06 / Area for display and activities
07 / Expanded hall space for greenery
08 / Living room on third floor
09 / Backyard and patio

Section 1

Section 2

751 Fashion Buyer Shop

Location / Beijing, China
Area / 4628 square feet (430 square meters)
Completion / 2017
Design / CUN Design
Photography / Wang Ting, Wang Jin

The store is located in a fashion district renovated from old factories. The designers insisted that the design should serve the store's commercial purpose. The designers used a part of the display property used in a previous Beijing International Design Week.

Product display is not a purely artistic behavior, but shows the beauty of the products themselves and combines the products with a sales atmosphere. In order to moderate the industrial climate, designers selected some materials close to daily life for the display installations, such as red brick, wood, and concrete. These are the main materials in the daily life in the past 30 years most closely related with customers. Color is a trigger to generate the feelings about space. The central area in pure white is the core of the display, creating a contrast with the surrounding dark blue. Attracted by the strong visual impact, customers are lured into the space. A floor-to-ceiling window was set on one side of the central area, extinguishing the new and old space, combining them together. The corridor outside the window became the fashion runway when fashion shows area held.

The capacity of the space is limited. Thus, buffer space exists between displaying products and original structure. The designers handled the relationships between people, objects, sounds, and colors by endowing them all with aesthetic value.

01 / Product display area

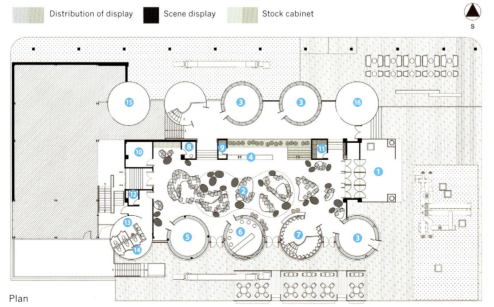

Distribution of display   Scene display   Stock cabinet

N
S

① Entrance
② Product display area
③ Brand display area
④ Checkout counter
⑤ Fashion show area
⑥ Café
⑦ Reading area
⑧ Locker room
⑨ Audio control room
⑩ Equipment room
⑪ Management room
⑫ Cleaning room
⑬ Men's restroom
⑭ Women's restroom
⑮ Warehouse
⑯ Hidden storage room

Plan

02 / View from exterior
03 / Passage
04 / Checkout counter

Original scheme

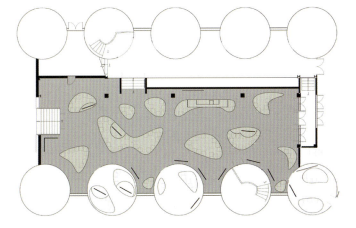

Total opening area of store: 2982 square feet (277 square meters)
Area of display items: 678 square feet (63 square meters)
Vacant area: 2303 square feet (214 square meters)

Current scheme

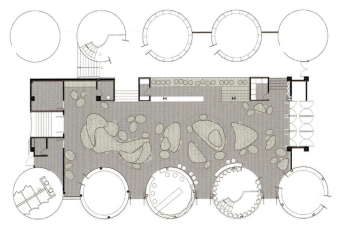

Total opening area of store: 3197 square feet (297 square meters)
Area of display items: 786 square feet (73 square meters)
Vacant area: 2411 square feet (224 square meters)

05 / Product display area
06 / Details of display items
07 / View towards display area from passage
08 / Display table

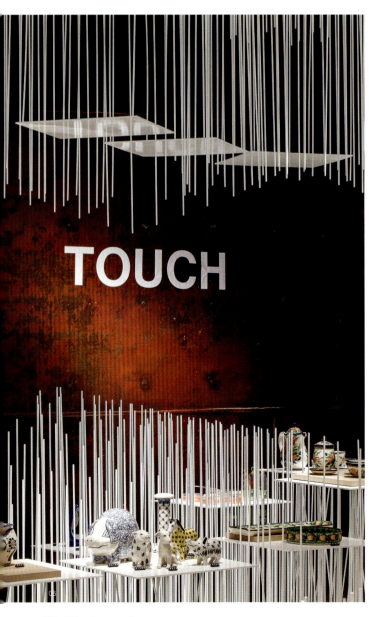

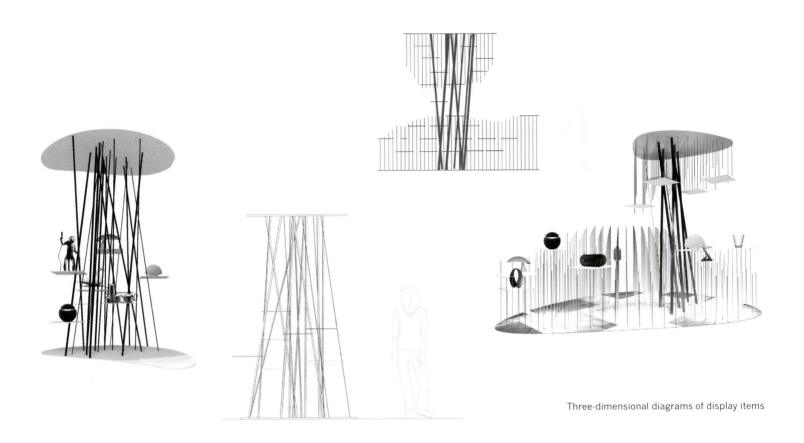

Three-dimensional diagrams of display items

09–10 / Product display area
11 / Reading area

Runner Camp Flagship Store

Location / Shanghai, China
Area / 6921 square feet (643 square meters)
Completion / 2017
Design / PRISM DESIGN, OFFICE Coastline
(cooperative design)
Photography / Makoto Adachi, Alessandro Wang

The theme of design was 'urban athletics,' a theme aimed at advocating a healthy yet fashionable lifestyle. The staircase was the focal point of the design. The two floors in the store respectively represent the east and west part of Shanghai and are connected with the central stairs, thus symbolizing athletics connecting the whole city.

Designers selected metal grids, acoustic fiber boards, heat insulation materials, and concrete to be used for the walls. Metallic materials give off an industrial feeling. However, the presentation is still fashionable, with the use of materials like orange acrylic, stainless steel wires, and frosted metal boards. The use of metal grids as display shelves that can be easily moved combines function and aesthetics.

The two floors of the shop were connected with the new stairs, allowing for new functions. The first floor is used for sales, while the second floor is open to many more functions, including professional sport training, which has an LED screen and exercising space; a shower room; and supporting facilities. The store is meant to be a central camp for runners. Most runners in city like to come out at drawn or dusk. The first color that would jump into people's minds about these two times of the day is orange. Being an energetic color, orange is a nice choice to be the brand's color. For all the customers coming to the store, designers hoped to convey to them the brand's central concept: an urban, healthy, and avant-garde lifestyle being advocated and formed in Shanghai.

01 / Central stairs

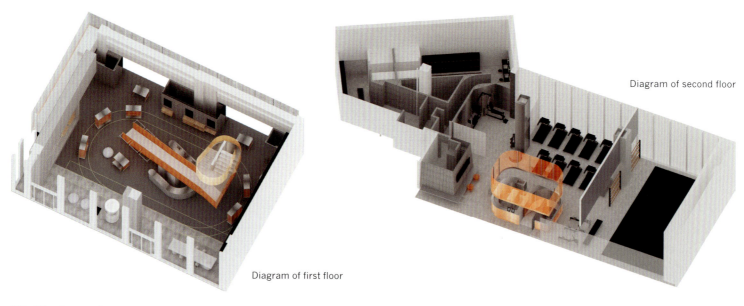

Diagram of second floor

Diagram of first floor

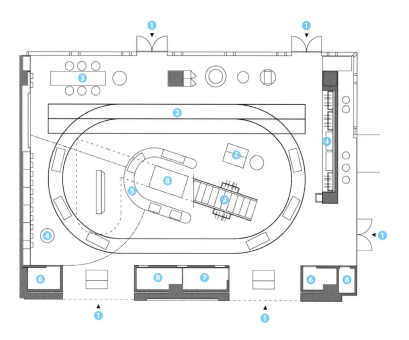

First-floor plan

1. Entrance
2. Running test zone
3. Consulting bar
4. Display area
5. Counter
6. Changing room
7. Staff room
8. Storage
9. Staircase

02–04 / Display area on first floor
05 / Product display

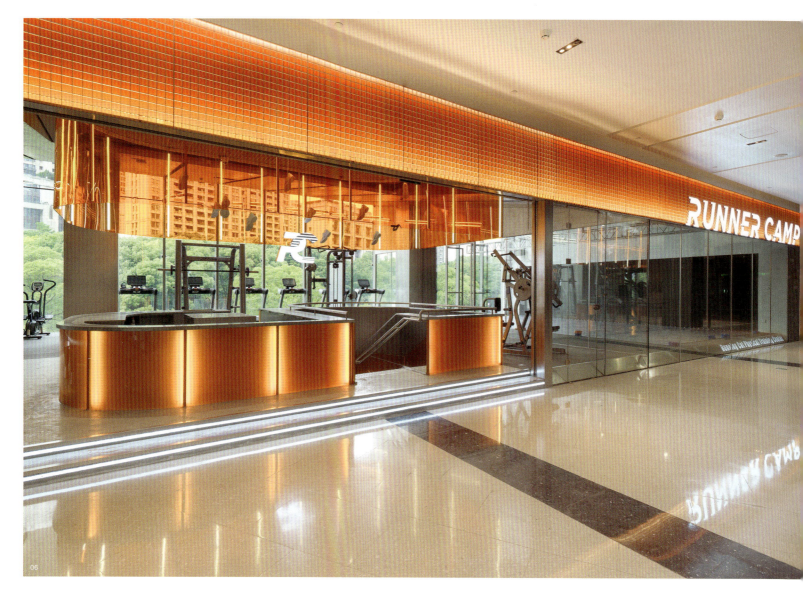

06–07 / Runner camp
08 / LED screen and exercise space
09 / Area for rest and storage

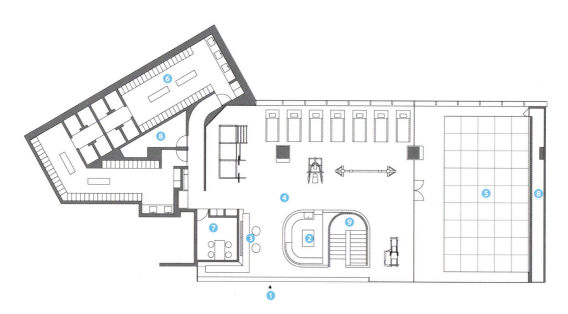

Second-floor plan

① Entrance
② Counter
③ Rest space
④ Gym
⑤ LED floor
⑥ Locker room
⑦ Staff room
⑧ Equipment room
⑨ Staircase

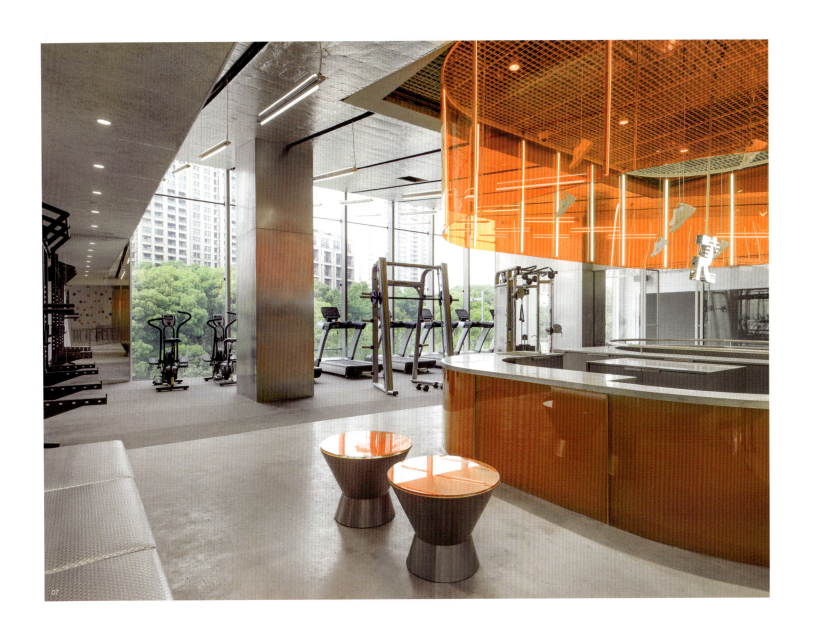

07

08

09

INDEX

MVRDV
P. 198

Web: www.mvrdv.nl
Email: office@mvrdv.com
Tel: 0031 010 477 2860

NONEZONE Space Atelier
P. 186

Web: www.nanzhudesign.com
Email: nanzhudesign@163.com
Tel: 0086 133 3877 7531

Normann Copenhagen
P. 142

Web: www.normann-copenhagen.com
Email: normann@normann-copenhagen.com
Tel: 0045 3555 4459

OEO Studio
P. 42

Web: www.oeo.dk
Email: info@oeo.dk
Tel: 0045 7021 7080

OFFICE Coastline
P. 232

Web: www.officecoastline.com
Email: contact@officecoastline.com

OOS
P. 100

Web: www.oos.com
Email: press@oos.com
Tel: 0041 435 005 005

Paulo Martins Arq&Design
P. 88

Web: www.paulomartins.com.pt
Email: geral@paulomartins.com.pt
Tel: 00351 910 014 252

PRISM DESIGN
P. 232

Web: www.prismdesign.com
Email: dbo@prismdesign.com

PRODUCE WORKSHOP PTE LTD
PP. 158, 208

Web: www.produce.com.sg
Email: enquiry@produce.com.sg
Tel: 0065 6846 8273

PUMP DESIGN Ltd.
P. 24

Web: www.pumpo.cn
Email: pumpocnppb@163.com
Tel: 0086 0571 8617 3386

PYO arquitectos
P. 170

Web: www.pyoarquitectos.com
Email: info@pyoarquitectos.com
Tel: 0034 91 012 0747

Shishang Architecture
P. 68

Web: www.shishangarchitecture.com
Email: info@shishangarchitecture.com

SkB Architects
P. 96

Web: www.skbarchitects.com
Email: info@skbarchitects.com
Tel: 001 206 903 0575

SOMA
P. 46

Web: www.soma.us
Email: mail@soma.us
Tel: 001 917 912 6007

Studio Ardete Pvt Ltd.
P. 36

Web: www.studioardete.com
Email: info@studioardete.com
Tel: 0091 (0)172 40 20 185

Studio Arthur Casas
P. 92

Web: www.arthurcasas.com
Email: press@arthurcasas.com
Tel: 0034 5511 2182 7500

studio mk27
P. 136

Web: www.studiomk27.com
Email: info@studiomk27.com.br
Tel: 0055 11 3081 3522

SuperLimão Studio
PP. 124, 130

Web: www.superlimao.com.br
Email: deux@superlimao.com.br
Tel: 0055 11 3518 8919

+tongtong
P. 54

Web: www.tongtong.co
Email: info@tongtong.co
Tel: 001 416 504 6563

TRIPTYQUE
P. 154

Web: www.triptyque.com
Email: triptyque@triptyque.com
Tel: 0055 11 3081 3565

TUX
P. 60

Web: www.tux.co
Email: hello@tux.co
Tel: 001 (514) 664 5722

Zooco Estudio
P. 104

Web: www.zooco.es
Email: zooco@zooco.es
Tel: 0034 942 030 921

Published in Australia in 2018 by
The Images Publishing Group Pty Ltd
Shanghai Office
ABN 89 059 734 431
6 Bastow Place, Mulgrave, Victoria 3170, Australia
Tel: +61 3 9561 5544 Fax: +61 3 9561 4860
books@imagespublishing.com
www.imagespublishing.com

 A catalogue record for this
book is available from the
National Library of Australia

Title: Store Design: Experience-Based Retail
Author: Brendan MacFarlane (ed.)
ISBN: 9781864708042

Printed by Everbest Printing Investment Limited, in Hong Kong/China